HOW TO SCORE

Science and the Beautiful Game

KEN BRAY

Granta Books

London

Granta Publications, 2/3 Hanover Yard, Noel Road, London N1 8BE

First published in Great Britain by Granta Books 2006

A CIP catalogue record for this book is available from the British Library.

1 3 5 7 9 10 8 6 4 2

ISBN-13: 978-1-86207-832-1
ISBN-10: 1-86207-832-7

Typeset by M Rules

Printed and bound in Italy by Legoprint

To Susan, for her encouragement and unfailing optimism.

ACKNOWLEDGEMENTS

Anyone writing about football, especially the scientific found-ations of the modern game, faces a problem. Not much exists as a written record before the early 1950s, when the game was ruled by tradition and technical innovation was reported largely in anecdotal format. I have therefore drawn heavily on Morris Marples' scholarly *A History of Football* in describing the early game in England, and on Brian Glanville's witty and erudite *The Story of the World Cup* for insights into the international dimen-sion. Rogan Taylor and Andrew Ward's *Kicking and Screaming: An Oral History of Football in England* has also been a rich inspiration, especially for insights into football's cultural and technical evolu-tion by players and coaches. The psychology of sport is a more recent discipline, perhaps not yet fully assimilated into main-stream football. I have found John H. Kerr's *Rethinking Aggression and Violence in Sport* invaluable for the insight it provides into violence in the modern game.

These and other sources I have used are quoted in the biblio-graphy where I have taken what might seem to be an unusual step in including scientific references in a popular work. This may be less painful than confronting the reader with mathe-matical equations in the text, although I hope a few will not be deterred from digging deeper. A good starting point for those so inclined would be Thomas Reilly and A. Mark Williams' comprehensive collection of review articles in *Science and Soccer*: Not bedtime reading but one of the best accounts of modern football science in all its complexity.

My special thanks go to Peter Tallack of Conville and Walsh, who provided the practical inspiration for *How to Score* and to Bella Shand of Granta who patiently guided me through the editorial essentials of producing a finished manuscript.

Above all I must record my debt to David Kerwin, Professor of Biomechanics at the University of Wales Institute, Cardiff. David's biomechanical insights have tempered many of my more extravagant theoretical speculations in our joint research although some have taken wing. Wild ideas sketched out on paper napkins in university cafeterias still have a place in scientific work and David will recognise many of the strands in the narrative that follows.

Ken Bray, Bath 2005

CONTENTS

INTRODUCTION

Football in today's recognisable form has been played for nearly 150 years. From obscure beginnings it has grown into the world's most popular game, played by 240 million people in 200 countries around the globe. Major tournaments such as the World Cup attract television audiences reckoned in billions, more than for any other sport. The pace of change has been rapid over this period, although many of the innovations that make today's spectacle have occurred in only the last 50 years or so. Some changes have been for the worse. Compared with the Corinthian ideals – that is, the gentleman amateur values – of the clubs who formed the early Football Association in England in the 1860s, football has a harder professional edge wherever it is now played. There was originally no need for referees; captains resolved disputes in amicable discussion despite the fact that the early game was much more robustly physical than today's, and would agree punishments for playing infringements such as deliberate fouls. There were no formal sanctions for foul play originally because no player would set out with such a nefarious purpose in mind. When the penalty kick was introduced in 1891 some goalkeepers would refuse to attempt a save, in protest at their team mate's unsporting behaviour in fouling an opponent to prevent a goal. Compare this with the antics that surround penalty shoot-outs in today's game, or the intimidation of referees who make controversial decisions.

Commercialism more than any other factor has driven the

changes in football at the top level. Anyone who doubts this should look at the financial returns (Deloitte and Touche Sport, 2005) for the 'top five' in European football (the English Premiership and equivalent senior leagues in Italy, Germany, Spain and France). In the 2003–04 season, revenues grossed £3.9 billion. The average figure for Italy, Germany, Spain and France was £638 million each and in England alone it was £1.3 billion, double that of the other four countries. Of the £1.3 billion for the English game, something like 45 per cent was accounted for by receipts from television deals, in what has accurately been called a '100 per cent profit-margin business'. Paying spectators – the fans – contributed £395 million in England through ticket sales. They also bought £100 million worth of replica shirts, a highly profitable merchandising activity given the frequency with which a team's playing strip is changed nowadays.

And yet, despite the cynical commercial aspects of the game, its appeal remains its fundamental simplicity. For most of football's early development in the nineteenth century the innovations were made by relatively few individuals, players and coaches who thought deeply about the game's basic nature. Modern playing formations evolved largely in response to modifications to the early offside rule, still a topic of controversy today. These changes were responsible for transforming the Victorian game from an individualistic, dribbling frenzy into the passing team game familiar to modern spectators. But locked into the very nature of stringing a series of passes together is an iron rule, one of the hidden rules of football that would not be appreciated until quantitative science began to be applied to the game in the 1960s. It is a very simply stated statistical fact: your chances of pulling off a sequence of continuous passes falls away rapidly the longer the movement goes on, and more than six is very rare even at the top level. This statement is often met with incredulity; everyone can cite that marvellous sequence of eight passes, possibly more, that ended with a spectacular goal. The problem is that memory is very selective, and instantly forgotten is the mountain of dross in the average game involving tedious exchanges where the ball is given away, or won after a single pass or two. It is the quality, not quantity, of the passing and its execution that matters in the final stages. When the pitch is divided into thirds along its length – the so-called defending, middle and attacking thirds – research shows that 80 per cent of all goals result from three or fewer consecutive passes in the attacking third and over 60 per cent are scored from possessions won in this part of the pitch. Most curious of all in the professional game is the ratio of goals scored to shooting attempts. Whenever the ratio is measured the conversion rate comes out at between one in nine and one in ten, but no one knows why this should be so.

Findings like these led to much controversy when many observers refused to accept that statistical chance played any part in such an apparently purposeful game. In 1969, an article by the sports editor of *The Times* summed up the views of the dissenters. Its headline read: 'Pins are better than form on the football pools.' This ridiculed the formal research by drawing a comparison between the scientific findings and the many millions who hoped to win a fortune on 'the pools', a form of gambling where participants had to select eight teams in the English and Scottish leagues that would draw their games. Serious entrants studied past form, but many fortune-winners confessed to picking out the teams blindfold by sticking a pin into the fixture list. The *Times* article rather snidely compared statistical match analysis with pin-sticking but such views were brushed aside by a handful of coaches who were sold on the ideas, and who responded to statistical data on passing by producing the effective, if unappealing, 'direct' or 'long ball' game. This was based firmly on the idea that delivering the ball into the attacking third with as little ceremony as possible was the route to scoring goals, and some teams became expert at this in the English domestic game.

Statistical research was quickly enhanced when techniques drawn from many other branches of science were applied to football in the 1960s, and football science has since become an essential tool in understanding and developing the game. My own interest in the science that lies behind football began at that time. It seemed to me that the swerving free kick was as legitimate a topic for theoretical physics as problems in quantum mechanics. This spectacular way of beating the defensive wall was just becoming established in the European game following its earlier introduction in South America. What could possibly be going on in the fleeting eight-tenths of a second between the shot and the goal that could modify the ball's trajectory so spectacularly? I consulted one of the England players who had competed in the epic World Cup final at Wembley in 1966. My question was simple: why does the ball so often end up ballooning over the bar when an inexperienced player takes the shot? I was inching towards the idea that spin was the determining factor, implying that top players were using this mechanism, consciously or not, in bringing off spectacular free kicks. He thought for a moment and said, 'It's because the ball is light and full of air, so it loves to rise.'

I was so taken aback by this bizarre answer that I did a simple experiment to discover if there was anything behind his interpretation. All I needed was a pump, a pressure gauge and a sensitive weighing balance. Theoreticians are not supposed to go into the lab as they have a tendency to break things, so I ran the gauntlet of my experimental colleagues and endured much leg-pulling, but the answer was easily obtained. To inflate a match ball to regulation pressure takes only 7 gm of air, less than 2 per cent of the ball's weight. Nor, given its regulation weight of between 397 and 454 gm (14–16 oz), is a ball especially light. Correct inflation is essential for the ball's resilience in a bounce and also in ensuring a regular aerodynamic shape as it speeds through the air, but as far as making it rise is concerned, the air it contains is absolutely irrelevant. The unwanted effect that makes it rise uncontrollably is the aerodynamic force caused by backspin, always to be avoided in a free kick. In the event I ended up little wiser about the science of a swerving shot than my adviser at that time. The mathematical equations describing the flight of a spinning football were easy to formulate but solving them with 1960s-vintage computers was another matter. And to have accurately measured the ball's position in three dimensions in an experimental free kick in order to test correctly the theory of ball spin would have been a practical impossibility at that time.

The field has grown considerably since the 1960s and while there are still some sceptics who feel that the phrase 'sports science' is a contradiction in terms, others take an enlightened view. In at least one discipline, human physiology – the science of the mechanical, physical and biochemical functions of life – the contribution of sports scientists is vital. Sports commentators often say that the game has become much less physical, meaning that less and less contact is allowed between players competing for possession of the ball. In fact, the opposite is the case: physical contact may be limited but the demands of the game in terms of the stress placed on body metabolism have magnified as the intensity of play has increased. In a match that goes into extra time a midfielder who stays on for the full 120 minutes can expect to run approaching 13 kilometres (8 miles). This is not a jog in the park; throughout that period the player will be operating at an average level of 75 per cent of the body's maximum aerobic capacity, the mechanism responsible for transporting oxygen to the active muscle cells to fuel the physical exertion. This should be compared with a figure of only 6 per cent, which is a fit athlete's resting aerobic energy requirement. For short intensive bursts the metabolism will be stressed beyond the maximum aerobic limit and finite energy reservoirs must be plundered in the muscle groups themselves, so-called anaerobic sources. Professional clubs retain physiologists to quantify these requirements on a player-by-player basis and, more importantly, to determine the nutritional requirements for restoring energy levels, often almost completely drained after hard matches.

Similar examples could be drawn from many related areas in the field. Look at any of the scientific journals dedicated to sport and you will find contributions from such diverse disciplines as physics, mathematics, biology, physiology, biomechanics, computing science and psychology. Football in all its codes (Rugby football, Gaelic football, Australian Rules football, etc.) is reviewed in the literature, although Association football dominates and the game and players have greatly benefited from this applied research. There is even a World Congress on Science and Football, held every four years since 1987, bringing together all parties with an interest in quantitative research in this field. It was first held in Liverpool, and the venues have been as diverse as Eindhoven, Cardiff, Sydney and Lisbon.

In the chapters that follow I address the broad theme of science and football, starting with football's history, not simply to recount an often fascinating story but to show how the game was shaped by the constraints under which it was originally played. Science is then used to illuminate the evolution of playing tactics and reveal how elite footballers have exploited aerodynamics in producing spectacular free kicks. Football's moves then go under the microscope, starting with the studies that first revealed the energy players expend in various positions, leading to the impact that these findings have had on fitness and nutrition. Another growing scientific field is the psychology of sport. The game is often won or lost in the mind, underlining the importance of correct psychological preparation. Football's basic skills, kicking, heading and throwing, are then reviewed, leading to an analysis of set pieces such as penalties and free kicks, the 'games within the game'. Finally, I take a look at the future; not the distant future but developments on the horizon, such as technology to resolve goal-line incidents and artificial playing surfaces, now making a serious comeback at the top level of football.

Some readers may feel surprised that there is so much to say about science in the development of football. Others might argue that its presence in what Pelé called 'the beautiful game' is an intrusion; football according to this view is an art, and close scientific scrutiny diminishes it as a spectacle. It is an old argument.

The poet John Keats bemoaned Newton's explanation that a rainbow was a mere spectrum of colours, and in his poem 'Lamia' asked, 'Do not all charms fly at the mere touch of cold philosophy?' Philosophy in Keats' era meant science, perhaps not quite the science of laboratories and computer analysis that we recognise today, but his criticism is echoed by modern dissenters and I think it overlooks the great advantages that science can confer. None of the game's grace and purpose is undermined by scientific insights; instead, as football's hidden rules are revealed, our enjoyment can only increase. Let us apply a little cold philosophy to football; the game can take it.

CHAPTER 1

EARLY DAYS – FROM MOB FOOTBALL TO THE GROWN-UP GAME

Football's roots can be traced directly to a raucous, violent game played originally in the towns and villages of medieval England. Four surviving descendants of these early contests give us an idea of what went on. They are the Shrove Tuesday games still played at Alnwick in Northumberland, Ashbourne in Derbyshire, Atherstone in Warwickshire and Sedgefield in Durham. One hundred and fifty years ago the list was much longer and there are records of Shrovetide football at such places as Derby, Scarborough, Whitby, Twickenham and London, to name a few. The ancient game was also played in Wales and the border region of eastern Scotland, and there are accounts of a related game called *la Soule*, played in Brittany and Normandy since the Middle Ages. *La Soule* died out in France towards the end of the eighteenth century, although it has enjoyed a limited modern revival. Football in Italy, *calcio*, has a similar, though younger, pedigree than the English and French medieval games and a traditional form was played in Florence during the Renaissance.

The rules of the Shrovetide matches, played once a year before Easter, were simple. Anyone from the local district could play, with team numbers often counted in the hundreds. In these traditional games goals were easily identifiable landmarks: a door or tree, or the porch of some prominent building. Sometimes neighbouring parishes competed, as St Paul's and St Michael's still do at Alnwick. In the Ashbourne game, where Up'ards play Down'ards, the distinction has always been one of birthplace. Up'ards are born north of the River Henmore, which forms part of the 'pitch'; Down'ards are born south of it. The goals in this game are stone plinths set three miles apart in the banks of the river, replacements for the original goal markers located at the mills of Sturston and Clifton.

The Ashbourne game has been played since at least the Middle Ages and good records have survived from 1891 to the present day. Browsing the statistics over the years makes interesting reading. Only the countryside restrictions caused by foot-and-mouth disease in 1968 and 2001 have prevented play. Each Shrove Tuesday and Ash Wednesday the ball is 'turned up' (thrown to the crowd) in the Shaw Croft car park and the free-for-all ensues. The game is played between 2 and 10 p.m. each day, the record for the fastest strike (traditionally called a 'goaling') standing at 30 minutes, which in a match lasting eight hours counts practically as a goal straight after the kick-off. There have been three disputed goals over the years, although how such incidents could even be recognised in the chaos of Shrovetide football, when the modern game is still struggling with the technology needed to resolve goal line disputes, is a mystery. There is one recorded 'own goal', in 1972, when a Down'ard gained possession and bizarrely scored for the opposition. His family is said to have ostracised him.

The league table for the 112 years' play is also revealing. The Up'ards just shade it with 75 wins to 71 and have the better goal-scoring record with 118 for, 108 against. Whether some form of transfer system operates is not clear, but perhaps the Down'ards, like Chelsea in the English Premiership, would benefit from a rich patron. Also interesting is the fact that spectators have seen, on average, one goal per game over the years. Not a bad record when one considers some of the sterile, ultra-defensive encounters thrown up by the modern game.

The Ashbourne ball is typical of the historical leather-cased models, but filled with cork to make it buoyant since it, and the players, invariably end up in the river. If you want an image of the traditional game think of a modern rugby scrum hugely expanded, with the ball hidden by hundreds of heaving, shoving bodies. Doubtless the opportunity was taken to settle a few old scores in the general mayhem and it is not surprising that there have been severe injuries, even deaths, over the years.

How football arrived in Britain is not an easy question to answer. The most likely candidate may be the game brought by the roman legions after the conquest in AD 43. Called *harpastum*, this was played with a small ball on a rectangular pitch with a centre line and two baselines. The broad objective was to throw the ball over the opponents' line by passing it from player to player. Tackling was very physical, players wrestling with one another for possession of the ball. There seem to have been recognised positions equating roughly to defenders and attackers and one key player, especially skilled, who was stationed near the middle of the pitch. He was called the '*medicurrens*' ('in-between man') and it is tempting to see his role as that of the modern midfield 'playmaker'. The Shrove Tuesday games may simply represent a primitive attempt to mimic *harpastum* and, if so, would point to a common source for the Shrovetide game in Britain and for the similar game, *la Soule*, in France.

There are claims, though, for more ancient ancestry. W. Branch Johnson, writing in the 1929 *Contemporary Review*, called football 'A Survival of Magic', and argued that the Shrove Tuesday games in England and France were the folk successors of a kind of sun ritual, enacted to ensure success in the harvest. The ball, naturally enough, represented the sun. At Scone in Scotland a goal was scored when one team succeeded in burying the ball in a defined location. The opponents had to 'drown' the ball by dipping it in a river. Both goals are located in the river banks at Ashbourne but at Scarborough the objective was to plunge the ball into the sea. Branch Johnson associates these actions with the warming of the earth (burying the ball, i.e. the sun) to ensure that seed would germinate and with rainfall to nurture the growing crop (dunking the ball in the river or sea). The struggle for the ball and its return to the home parish is interpreted as a contest to capture the sun, so securing a better harvest.

Today's soccer fans may scoff at these notions and argue that the Shrovetide kick-about was simply an opportunity to let off steam before the fasting and restrictions of Lent set in. We shall never know either way, but what is certain is that the game was firmly established by the twelfth century and played with gusto from the early Middle Ages onwards. The earliest written record dates from 1175 when William Fitzstephen reports a Shrove Tuesday game in London, probably at Smithfields. He calls it 'the famous game of ball' and describes the spectators as 'older men, fathers and men of property'.

There are also glimpses of the game's darker side. In 1280 Henry de Ellington was killed during a game at Ulgham in Northumberland when he and David le Keu collided violently. The inquest heard that le Keu's dagger was sheathed but nevertheless penetrated de Ellington's stomach in the impact. Misadventure was recorded. In 1321 William de Spalding, a cleric, killed his friend in exactly the same way. De Spalding was apparently so contrite that he sought and obtained a dispensation from the Pope. The cynic might question whether sheathed daggers could really have inflicted such terrible wounds and argue that they were in reality drawn, as tempers ran out of control in the violent clashes between the players. The problem was not confined to the English game: there were many similar requests for papal absolution following games of *la Soule* in France, albeit for 'broken heads' rather than stabbings.

This player violence, probable injury to innocent bystanders and certain damage to property prompted many official bans on the sport. These extended from the fourteenth to the seventeenth centuries. Royal proclamations were issued from Edward II's to

Henry VIII's reigns and there were many by what we would now call the local authorities. In a strange twist Edward II was buried in Gloucester Cathedral, close to possibly the world's first image of football, a woodcarving celebrating the game he did his best to suppress.

Fig. 1.1: Traditional footballers, Gloucester Cathedral, c. 1340

The carving (Fig. 1.1) dates from *c.* 1340 and is located underneath one of the seats in the choir, just a few steps from Edward's ornate tomb. It shows two young footballers enjoying the game, an image drawn perhaps from the carver's own experience of football in medieval Gloucester. What is amazing is that nearly seven centuries ago he depicted what the game would become, a skilled and athletic contention for the ball, rather than the mayhem and violence of mob football of the time. This image gives some idea of how much football had become part of everyday life and the popular resentment of all the royal and official edicts that would follow. Richard II's version, issued in 1388, clearly identifies the target groups. It decrees that '. . . servants and labourers shall have bows and arrows and use the same on Sundays and holidays, and leave all playing at ball . . . and other such importune games'.

The mention of Sundays and holidays shows that by as early as the fourteenth century the game had broken free of the once-a-year Shrovetide encounters and gives a clear picture of the social class – labourers and servants – with whom the game was popular and who, in the official view, should have been devoting free time to military training. Henry VIII's was the last royal ban, possibly disingenuous on his part as he apparently enjoyed playing football and even commissioned a special pair of boots for his hobby. No succeeding monarch thought it necessary to revise his wording, though, and his statute prevailed until 1845 as 'The bill for maintaining artillery and the debarring of unlawful games'.

From the beginning of the sixteenth century onwards the emphasis shifted; less is heard about military training and more about the socially disruptive aspects of the game. It came under severe and sustained threat from the Puritans, who reserved special displeasure for Sunday football. In 1583 Philip Stubbes, a well-known Puritan kill-joy, imagines in his writings a dialogue between pupil and mentor where the odious youngster asks, 'Is the playing of football, reading of merry books, and suchlike delectations, a violation or prophanation of the Sabbath Day?' The mentor weighs in with a list of football's failings, among them 'fighting, brawling contentions, quarrel-picking, murder, homicide and great effusion of blood'. There is no evidence that Stubbes' tirades had any effect on the popularity of football; players were undeterred and the game flourished. There are indications, though, that the authorities were beginning to act. The players were obvious targets but in 1610 two spectators were prosecuted for watching a Sunday game in Bedford. The players, being fitter, presumably made a run for it. More bizarrely, in 1616 at Guisborough in Yorkshire, a man was brought before the magistrates, not for playing or watching, but for 'making a banquet for football players on the Sabbath'. Fines were levied. In 1647 at Hexham in Northumberland, the penalty was two shillings for Sunday play, about a day and a half's wages for a skilled craftsman at that time. How many successful prosecutions were brought and how much paid in fines is unknown, but spectators, players and caterers were clearly willing to run the risk.

Not all opinion was negative. Richard Mulcaster, the first headmaster of Merchant Taylors' School, writing just two years before Stubbes' broadside, praised football and argued for its positive effect on pupils' health and education. He was scathing, however, about the popular game, its 'thronging of a rude multitude, with bursting of shins and breaking of legs'. He went on to make the suggestion, astonishing for its time, that the game would benefit from having a 'smaller number of players . . . sorted into sides and standings'. Even more radically, he suggested that there should be a 'training master' and someone who 'can judge of the play, and is judge over the parties, and has the authority to command'. These are almost perfect descriptions of the roles of team coach and referee. Sadly, Mulcaster's views were ignored for more than two centuries and there is no evidence to show that the popular game developed in any technical sense in the intervening period, either in the wider community or in the schools.

In the eighteenth and nineteenth centuries efforts to suppress football became more determined. At Beverley in Yorkshire in 1825, local constables failed to stop a game and were roughly treated. Arrests followed and sentences of hard labour for the offenders proved an effective deterrent. It was not until the formation of Peel's police force in 1839, however, that the authorities could rely on permanent law enforcers to control unacceptable public behaviour. No matter how popular the game remained in some quarters, the decisive factor in most people's view was the affront to public order. Provincial towns were growing and an increasingly enlightened population became less and less tolerant of what they saw as mob violence played out in congested streets. In some instances, as at Derby in 1847, the authorities were so determined to suppress the game that they backed up the police by calling in mounted troops as reserves. When the players refused to disperse, the Riot Act was read by the mayor and the desired effect achieved: no one wanted to face a determined cavalry charge. In 1819 the Manchester Yeomanry had broken up a peaceful assembly at St Peter's field in Manchester with drawn sabres, killing 11 and wounding 400. This came to be called 'the Peterloo Massacre', after the Battle of Waterloo, and would have registered strongly in the public mind.

Measures like these were highly effective. The popular game was rapidly marginalised and began its decline. Today's surviving examples reflect some sort of local tolerance or practical accommodation following negotiation between players and the authorities. At Atherstone, Sedgefield and Ashbourne the game continues in the streets, still disruptive but much reduced in violent conflict compared with its medieval predecessors. In 1828 the Duke of Northumberland, who traditionally provided the ball for the Alnwick match, persuaded the players to transfer from the town to a plot of land north of the river, and this has been the venue for the game ever since.

Despite more than seven centuries of recorded history, football – which had defied royal injunctions, Puritan censure and municipal disfavour, and had shrugged its shoulders at considerable bloodshed, injury and even fatalities – faced extinction by early Victorian times. The tradition survived, as today's rare examples show, in an antiquarian curiosity which in sporting terms led to an absolute dead-end. What we enjoy today is the medieval game's successor, descend from the same evolutionary line. No one in the early nineteenth century, however, could have foreseen that football would be rescued in the unlikely quarter of the English public schools, where a pastime for schoolboys would flourish and ultimately be transformed into the world's most popular game.

School football in the early 1800s, played in nearly all of the boys' public schools of the day, had much in common with the Shrovetide game, but its development was strongly influenced by the pupils' own inclinations and inventiveness. They were the sons of the aristocracy and the aspiring middle classes, emphatically not the 'labourers and servants' identified in Richard II's ban of football. No doubt they would have seen the traditional game when they returned home in school holidays and some may even have joined in the local mayhem. At school, left to their own devices outside the classroom, they introduced a form of football markedly different in style. It was played with much more purpose and clearly according to agreed rules. Paradoxically, these rules developed from the restrictions imposed by the school environment, never a serious restraint in the traditional game. How, for example, was play to be restarted when the ball was out of bounds, and how exactly was a goal to be scored? More than any other factors, the rules of school football and their development over time began the processes that would lead ultimately to the modern game.

The first and most obvious constraint was space. At Charterhouse, football was originally played in paved cloisters 70 yards long and 4 yards wide (64 × 3.7 metres). At Winchester the pitch measured 80 by 27 yards (73 × 25 metres). The Eton Wall Game, still football despite all its apparent eccentricities, was played on a pitch 120 by 6 yards (110 × 5.5 metres). The Eton Field Game, played by the majority of the pupils, eventually settled on a pitch 130 by 90 yards (119 × 82 metres). All of these 'pitches', excluding Eton's Field Game, would fit into the maximum modern playing area of 120 by 80 yards (110 × 75 metres) and Eton's would be only just outside. Other schools – Harrow, Rugby, Shrewsbury and Westminster – played very much to their own codes. Goals were sometimes well defined, as in the Field Game at Eton where posts stood 11 feet (3.4 metres) apart and 7 feet (2.1 metres) high but without a crossbar. At Westminster the game was played in the Great Dean's Yard and trees at either end, conveniently 20 yards (18 metres) apart, served the purpose. At Rugby the posts defined a goal line of 11 feet, just as at Eton, but a crossbar was added 10 feet (3 metres) from the ground. The strangest goals were at Harrow and Winchester. At Harrow, posts 12 feet (3.7 metres) high were separated by 150 yards (137 metres) and if a match remained tied after a day's play the goal distance was doubled. At Winchester the whole of the 27-yard (25-metre) baseline at either end of the pitch defined the goal and earlier in the game's development there, young boys, or 'fags', were themselves used as posts. To score, a player had to drive the ball between their outstretched legs. The fags, who did menial tasks for their seniors and were routinely bullied, came in for a hard time of it. For school matches they would be sent out to play in defence, their only role to smother a ball that had broken clear of the brawling mass of seniors and was advancing dangerously, followed by the mob, towards goal.

These rules and conventions were for many years unwritten and simply handed down as oral tradition. Numbers of players in the early 1800s were not limited. In one match at Rugby, 40 boys from the sixth form (the most senior) took on 460 others; apparently, 200 of these played in the outfield with 260 keeping goal. As in Shrovetide football there were frequent scrimmages, where the players would brutally hack at one another's legs in an attempt to free the ball from the scrum. Hacking extended even to open play and players could be scythed down in an attempt to regain possession. In most schools the ball could be both handled and kicked, but running while carrying it was still in the future. The famous incident which gave rise to modern rugby was said to have occurred at Rugby School in 1823 when William Webb Ellis picked up the ball and ran with it. The story may not have much basis in fact, but no matter. What is clear is that the various codes and conventions differed in many important aspects but produced essentially two broad styles of play: one favoured dribbling the ball with minimal use of the hands; the other, significant handling and carrying. As long as the game was played in isolation there were no difficulties, but the differences were inevitably exposed when the factions met.

Clashes occurred first in the universities, where former public schoolboys continued to play the game, each version with its own differing code. In a game at Trinity College, Cambridge, in

1848, former Eton players, with their very restricted handling rules, bayed at the Rugby contingent who actually ran with the ball. Team sizes were also problematical; although these had reduced considerably by the mid-nineteenth century, it was still up to the captains to agree numbers (and rules), so games often started with 15 a side. By this time football had spread back into the community, where former schools players and graduates created the earliest clubs. Sheffield alone could boast 15 by 1862. There were so many different interpretations that something would have to be done. Mr Thring of Uppingham School produced one of the earliest attempts at a code of football, 'The Rules of the Simplest Game'. More serious were the deliberations at Cambridge between 1837 and 1863. This last meeting resulted in a set of rules favouring dribbling, since the committee that met that year was dominated by representatives from Eton, Harrow and Westminster, who played that way. The problems were ultimately resolved in another series of meetings involving representatives of 11 London clubs and schools. It is interesting to note that the majority were from the newly formed and increasingly popular community clubs where the representatives must have taken a more pragmatic view of the game, since they were now playing it as a leisure activity outside the purely school or university context.

The history has been told many times. The first of six meetings was on 26 October 1863 at the Freemasons Tavern in London. Unaware that there had been similar sessions in Cambridge, the parties formed themselves into the Football Association. Differences soon surfaced between the factions, however. Surprisingly, it was not a disagreement on carrying or handling the ball but the brutal practice of hacking that produced the eventual split. Their first attempts at a draft of the rules favoured the Rugby contingent and allowed hacking, but by the fourth meeting disquiet was being expressed. The Cambridge rules had surfaced and the dribblers in the Football Association were impressed at their censure of handling and hacking. It was an

important consideration to the many young men in the profes-
sions who were spreading the virtues of football in the
community, but did not relish returning badly kicked about to
their offices after a weekend game. The differences could not be
reconciled and so the hacking and carrying contingent seceded
and the game split into the two great codes: Rugby and
Association football (soccer). Ironically, hacking was quickly abandoned when the Rugby Union formalised its own code in 1871.

On 8 December 1863, 14 rules, issued by the newly formed
Football Association, said all there was to say about soccer. Rules
9 and 10 stated:

9.   No player shall carry the ball, and
10. Neither tripping nor hacking shall be allowed.

Both of the contentious issues which had divided the early association of clubs were now firmly resolved. There were some
strange throwbacks to the practice of hacking, however. In the
1870s some clubs allowed five minutes of this at the end of
matches, bizarrely referred to as a 'Hallelujah'. And in the first
international between England and Scotland in 1871, tempers
rose so high that both sides approached the referee requesting
that they be allowed to hack. He sternly refused and threatened
to walk off. The match played on, fully within the letter of the
Association code.

The 1863 rules addressed many other issues. Pitch dimensions
were fixed, setting the maximum length and breadth allowed at
200 by 100 yards (183 × 91 metres). This would later be reduced
to 130 by 100 yards (119 × 91 metres), a concession to today's
high work-rate midfielders who, fit though they are, would not
survive the 1863 challenge of repeatedly transiting 200 yards
between opposing penalty areas. Goals were marked by posts 8
yards (7.3 metres) apart, but explicitly excluded was 'any tape or
bar' to define the height. These rules would be revised and
improved over time, regulating everything from pitch markings to

throw-ins, from free kicks to penalties. But one rule, that for off-side, was more than any other to act as the catalyst for tactical development, profoundly shaping attacking and defensive play, and producing many unexpected results on the way. It is still being tinkered with today, with little discernible improvement in either understanding or enjoyment by officials and spectators alike.

A puzzle about the 1863 version of offside was that it reverted to a very restrictive form of the rule, played by the majority of the schools in the earlier epoch of the game. This placed a player off-side when he was closer to the opponents' goal line than the ball; passing to a team mate in a forward position was illegal but since the player in possession could not be offside – he was always behind the ball – tactics were reduced to frenzied, individual dribbling. Team mates fanned out behind, hoping for their moment of glory following a rare back pass or, more likely, a chance ricochet when the ball broke free. This style of play influenced teams' playing formations, which in the early 1870s looked very much like Fig. 1.2. There were 7 attackers (there had been as many as 9 originally) and 4 defenders, including the goal-

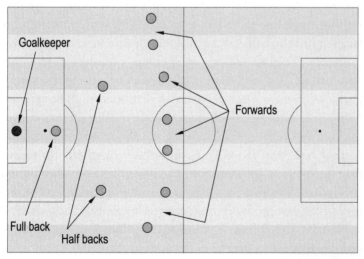

Fig. 1.2: Team formation, early 1870s

keeper. For the first time the goalkeeper's was a real position and he was the only player authorised to use his hands in defending the goal. As today though, how teams lined up had little to do with how they played, and we must imagine the forwards playing not in a line but 'backing up' the player in possession, looking for a loose ball to pounce on. Their support role also included shouldering opposing defenders away from the focus of the attack. Long, mazy dribbling runs in the classic English style were prized and stalwart players such as R. W. S. Vidal of Oxford University once got a hat trick without any opponent touching the ball between kick-off and scoring in each of his three goals. Given the numerical supremacy of forwards, this might be thought a very attacking formation. In fact scoring was difficult and, in modern terms, it would be considered ultra-defensive because of the ease and frequency with which offside could occur.

Perhaps this is why the rule was changed in 1867. According to the new definition, attackers were onside if three or more defenders, one of whom was usually the goalkeeper, were between them and the opponents' goal. Eton College had used just such a definition of offside in their Field Game and players who transgressed were described as 'sneaking'. Forward passing was now 'on' because players were not constrained to stay behind the ball. The tactic seems not to have occurred initially to English sides, or perhaps dribbling was too entrenched. The first team to exploit the new rule was Queen's Park of Glasgow. They played with distinction in the early FA Cup competitions, which began in the 1871–72 season, and are credited with invention of the passing game, an enormous tactical transformation for the time. In their formation (Fig. 1.3) one of the centre forwards (we can now begin to use this term) was removed, so that a second full back could be created. This was tactically important; a single full back and two half backs, the defensive shield in the older formation, could not be expected to neutralise the attacking movements of a side passing the ball intelligently. The six remaining forwards played

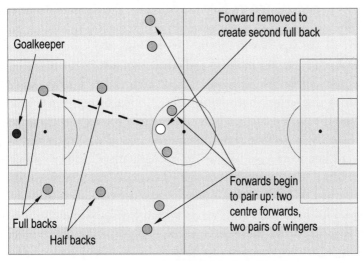

Goalkeeper

Forward removed to
create second full back

Full backs

Half backs

Forwards begin
to pair up: two
centre forwards,
two pairs of wingers

Fig. 1.3: Creation of second full back, end 1870s

in pairs: two sets of wingers and two centre forwards. This formation had a much more balanced feel. Not only was forward play more incisive, but defending was recognised as an essential skill, not to be routinely allocated to make-weight players who were simply not good enough to play up in attack. Queen's Park never won the FA Cup but their game was so dominant that between 1867 and 1875 no goals were scored against them. Their style was greatly admired then emulated by some of the English sides they played against, notably the Royal Engineers and the Sheffield clubs, and the dribbling game gradually withered away. The skill, though, remained, reinvested in wing play where these forwards were expected to be fast and able to take on the full backs, who increasingly specialised in defence.

So successful had the passing game become that by 1883 a further tactical innovation was introduced. Attackers could exploit the offside rule of 'three last defenders' by moving forward in anticipation of a pass, what we would nowadays call 'running into space'. It became imperative to time the defence-splitting pass to perfection or to hold the ball until the opening occurred. This required someone who could read the game intimately and see all the options available. One of the two centre forwards dropped back into midfield and was designated 'centre half'. This would not be the only occasion when a centre forward would adopt a so-called 'deep-lying' role, playing behind the forward line. It would recur in a watershed match between England and Hungary in 1953 and on many future occasions when the forward line would be depleted to strengthen midfield or defence. In this first incarnation, though, the centre half was the pivotal midfield playmaker, linking defence and attack. This left a forward line of 5 (Fig. 1.4), two of whom remained as out-and-out wingers; but in the middle three two players supporting the centre forward dropped back and began to play deeper, creating the role of inside forwards. This formation was often referred to as the 'classical pyramid'. The possibilities for moving the ball fluidly from defence to attack multiplied and football entered something of a golden era, much appreciated by the fans. It could

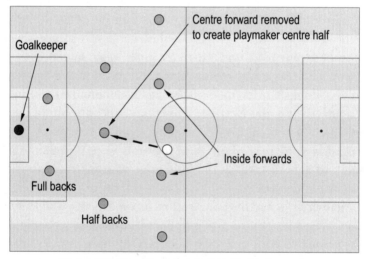

Fig. 1.4: The playmaker centre half and inside forwards:
'classical pyramid' formation, c. 1883

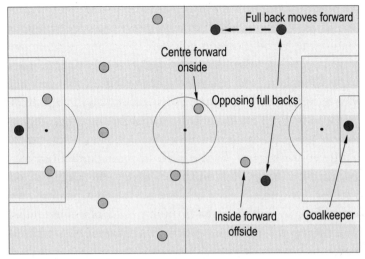

Fig. 1.5: Full backs exploiting the 'three defenders' offside rule.
Rule amended to two defenders in 1925

not last because full backs began to see how the 'last three defenders' offside rule could be exploited for purely defensive purposes. Why allow offside to occur spontaneously when it could be contrived by very simple positional manoeuvring on the pitch? Attacks could be very effectively broken down in this way and the game lurched into one of its negative phases.

A glance at Fig. 1.5 shows the problem. If one of the opposing full backs pushed forward, close to the advanced attackers, it was a simple matter to catch them in what came to be called the 'offside trap'. Careless forwards would then find only two defenders, the goalkeeper and the other full back, closer to goal than they were. This required timing and good understanding between the backs, but the tactic was highly effective. It killed the attacking dimension, however, and the game began to be played and strangled in what we would now call the 'middle third' of the field, with as many as 40 calls for offside per game. The solution, following debate at all levels of the game involving players, officials and fans, was to amend the offside rule once again. From 1925, the number of defenders between attacker and goal was reduced from three to two. The effect was immediate. The number of goals in the 1925–26 season increased by 30 per cent compared with the previous year. The advantage had swung back to attackers, who exploited the vulnerabilities of the final two defenders with relish. Defence-splitting passes – now called through-balls – swamped the full backs, and the forwards, the centre forward especially, had a field day.

The improved level of the coaches' technical understanding is indicated by the speed at which problems were identified, and resolved. One of the most astute was Herbert Chapman, who joined Arsenal in 1925 as the first full-time manager in football. He plugged the defensive gap by withdrawing the attacking centre half to a defensive position between the full backs (Fig. 1.6) in what became 'the third back' formation. This individual naturally came to be called the 'stopper' centre half, his role being that of nullifying the threat of the centre forward, cutting out through-balls, heading away crosses from the wings, and moving quickly to support a full back struggling against an

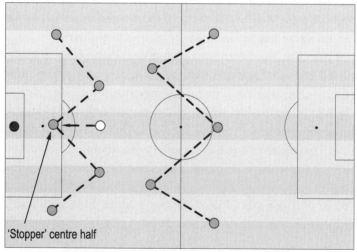

'Stopper' centre half

Fig. 1.6: Chapman's 'stopper' centre half and the 'W-M' formation, 1925

especially tricky winger. There was also an impact on the inside forwards, who played a little deeper to compensate for the loss of the creative centre half. English sides and many foreign teams quickly settled on this W-M formation, so called because playing positions resembled the shape of these letters on the field. It became almost universally popular as football spread throughout the world, but as we shall see, it was not the only tactical response, and much creative thinking about playing formations was evolving in Switzerland, Italy and especially Hungary.

Football from the 1920s to the 1950s had much in common with classical science as that discipline approached the end of the nineteenth century: both were at a zenith and it seemed that there was simply nothing left to discover in either field. Like classical science, football would proceed by steady refinement of the existing system, which was now numerically balanced between attack and defence. Full backs would continue to mark opposing wingers and the centre half and opposing centre forward would remain locked in a monumental struggle of headers and crunching tackles. England in particular had a proud record. Never beaten on home soil, they remained superior in their attitude to foreign opposition: let *them* worry about *us* was the maxim. All this would be swept away, just as classical science was superseded by the deeper insights of modern physics at the turn of the century. England's nemesis was waiting in the form of a gifted Hungarian team; one that would punish such complacency and, in ruthlessly exposing the defensive flaws of the carefully nurtured W-M formation, launch a new era of tactical development in football.

CHAPTER 2

HUNGARIAN RHAPSODY, OR PLAYING THE GAME BY NUMBERS

In 1953 England were punished as much for their tactical naïvety as for the flaws which lay at the very heart of the W-M playing system they had invented. The contrast between old and new was sharply drawn in two epic games played at Wembley Stadium that year. The first was the Cup Final between Blackpool and Bolton Wanderers in May, the second the friendly international between England and Hungary in November. It would be hard to find two games that so perfectly define the passing of an era: a Cup Final, generally acknowledged as the best ever, exhibiting all the virtues of the English game, and an international match just six months later where the national side's limitations would be cruelly exposed.

Arriving at the final of a knock-out competition such as the FA Cup is a little like evolution in miniature: teams are paired by random selection and the fittest, in theory, survive. The eliminating rounds of the 1953 competition eventually brought together Blackpool and Bolton Wanderers for the Wembley Final. Bolton had played in six previous finals, winning three – including the first to be played at the new Wembley Stadium in 1923. Blackpool, a team past its peak, had lost in 1948 and 1951, and for them there was a sense of time running out. So too for their veteran winger Stanley Matthews, capped many times for England but currently out of favour with the selectors and still without the FA Cup winner's medal every professional footballer covets. At 38 he was generally reckoned to be too old for the top flight. He confounded the doubters in this as in so many other things and played his last professional game aged over 50. His eventual knighthood, the first for a player, was thoroughly deserved, and recognition for his demeanour on and off the field as much as his playing ability.

Perhaps the Cup Final crowds and the millions watching on television deserved the spectacular match they saw in 1953. The previous year had closed with the worst smog on record as a stagnant, chemical blanket sat like a lid over the country for five days in December. Official figures gave the death toll as 4,000 but later estimates have shown this to be nearer 12,000. Then in January another hammer blow: a storm surge combined with a freak high tide and swept into the North Sea, breaching sea defences as far south as the Channel ports and the Netherlands. Over 2,000 lives were lost and many were left homeless. There was, then, a great sense of national relief when spring arrived. The population, like so many in Europe, was weary, tired of austerity, rationing and the grind of post-war reconstruction. The patriotic could look forward to street parties and flag-waving at the Coronation in June and football fans to the highlight of their year, the Wembley Final in May.

Both sides played W-M, the system that had proved its effectiveness for so many years. Looked at from today's perspective there were two serious flaws in the formation; these were rarely exploited because teams, certainly in domestic competition, effectively colluded with one another, rarely straying outside the prevailing tactical boundaries.

The first weakness concerned the rigidity of players' roles and the marking conventions that followed from them: centre halves marked centre forwards, full backs marked wingers and half backs marked inside forwards. It is difficult to appreciate today just how fixed these protocols were. Playing in that famous Cup

Final were two centre forwards in the classic mould, Nat Lofthouse for Bolton and Stan Mortensen for Blackpool. Both had distinguished careers as England internationals and both played an absolutely orthodox game, one-for-one against the opposing centre half in a succession of crunching headers and tackles. The idea that they might play behind the forward line instead of leading it would have seemed incongruous, just as it would if a full back of that era set off on a penetrating run, like a winger, deep into enemy territory. This may have happened on very rare occasions but such tactics were not part of the strategic mindset of most coaches of that day.

The second defect concerned the way in which defences in a W-M formation reacted to a developing attack. Teams playing this system built the 'M' on the basis of the centre half, two full backs and two defending half backs. Not until the attacking team had crossed the half-way line did the defence retreat, and then in a way that retained the shape of the formation, always provided that the attack was developing centrally (Fig. 2.1). This defence was often called 'balanced' or 'double-covered' because for such

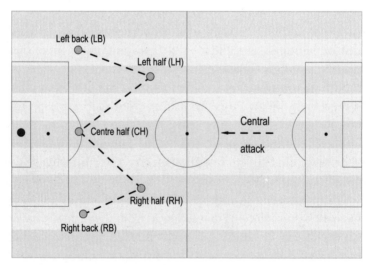

Fig. 2.1: The retreating 'M' in a W-M formation facing a central attack

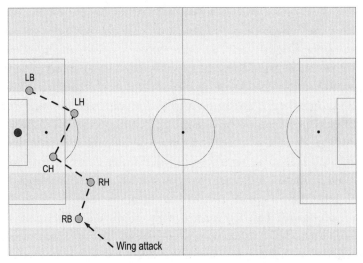

Fig. 2.2: The pivoted 'M' for an attack developing from the wing

attacks the most advanced defenders could rely on a team mate playing deeper to pick up any attacker who got past them. The problem came when attacks developed from wing positions; as today, wing 'assists' counted for a high proportion of goals scored in the 1950s. To maintain the double-cover principle the 'M' would swivel, with the centre half acting as the pivot (Fig. 2.2). The nearer full back would advance to the point of attack, which effectively dragged the 'M' away from the centre. The consequence was that the far full back was now defending much closer to his own goal line and pulled into a more central position. Forwards running through on the far side were less likely to be caught offside and a quick cross-field pass could exploit this. In such circumstances the defence was 'turned' as it faced up to the new attacking threat from the opposite side, a very bad prospect when the next move would very likely be a cross, or an attacking run, into the penalty area.

The 1953 Cup Final has become part of football's folklore. Bolton were strolling home at 3–1 up with only 22 minutes left. As in their two previous appearances, Blackpool seemed to have conceded – until Matthews began to work his magic. He was called the 'wizard of the dribble' but he was never a dribbler in the classic English style. His strength was speed off the mark. Sometimes he would receive the ball and wait a second or so at rest to compel the defender to come to him. Then he would move, not very quickly initially but in cadences, so that the defender would soon be retreating, running crab-wise, always watching Matthews over his shoulder. Next came the trademark body swerve; there would be a sideways feint where the ball would be shown and dragged with a leaning action of his body to the left, then a quick reversal of direction to unbalance the defender as the ball was pushed with the outside of the foot to the right, and past. Matthews would simply hit the ball forwards and take on the back in a sprint. Few were faster than he over 20 metres and the outcome of the encounter would usually see him cutting the ball back from near the dead-ball line, into the penalty area, perfectly placed for the forwards running in. His passing was immaculate and his centres, delivered with pin-point accuracy, invariably found the heads of the incoming forwards.

Many times in the closing minutes of that epic Final, Matthews received the dangerous cross-field pass, played into the space on the wing with the Bolton defence dangerously turned. We tend to forget that Bolton were hampered by injuries – these were the days before substitutes were allowed – but this should not detract from Matthews' performance. He roasted the Bolton defence; again and again the Bolton full back, fooled by Matthews' body swerve, 'bought the dummy'; and Blackpool were back to 3–3 with just three minutes to go. The winning goal came with almost the last kick of the game: Matthews pulled the ball back across the goal face from his favourite position near the dead-ball line and Bill Perry, running in, scored. Against all the odds, Blackpool had won it.

Asking whether Matthews' threat could have been neutralised that day seems like heresy. As easily neutralise the threat of a Cruyff, Pelé or Maradona playing – like Matthews – with sublime inspiration. Perhaps Bolton could have man-marked Matthews to cut out the initial supply and deny him space for his damaging runs. Or perhaps the long-suffering full back could have doubled up with another defender to counter Matthews' telling sprints to the dead-ball line. All such speculation is futile; that was the way the game was played and if it produced such a spectacle, what could possibly be wrong with English football? The answer would not be long in coming.

Later that May the England team toured in South America, a good opportunity for evaluating likely competition for the impending World Cup, to be held the following summer in Switzerland. World Cups were something of a novelty for England, given the FA's unhappy on-and-off affair with FIFA. This organisation, the Fédération Internationale de Football Association, was formed in May 1904 by Belgium, Denmark, France, the Netherlands, Spain, Sweden and Switzerland. A delegation sent to England to plead with the FA to take a leading role in the organisation was met with indifference; the FA, already four decades old, probably resented the presumption of these relatively junior organisations in setting up a controlling body for world football. But the English were won round almost a year later and joined in April 1905, graciously recognising the other nations affiliated to FIFA. The rift came in 1919, however, in the political fall-out after the First World War, when England and the other British Associations of Northern Ireland, Scotland and Wales withdrew. This isolation from the growing community of world football would cost British football dear as membership of FIFA was not renewed until 1946.

By 1953 then, England's experience of World Cup competitions was limited to one tournament, in 1950, when the team was beaten 1–0 by the United States in the qualifying rounds and never made it to the final stages. On their South America tour in 1953, however, England played virtually the best the continent had to offer in Argentina, Uruguay and Chile, although not, significantly, Brazil. They actually played Argentina twice, first against a representative Buenos Aires side (but in fact one containing virtually all the international players) then the full international side a few days later. They lost the first encounter 3–1, but drew 0–0 in the official game. The team performed well against Chile, defeating them 2–1, but foundered against a powerful Uruguay who won comfortably by the same score. Finally to New York, where full revenge was exacted for the 1950 World Cup shock. The US were comprehensively thrashed 6–3 and national pride was restored.

Based on the South American results, there were few reasons to doubt the team's ability and back home they prepared for a game celebrating the 90th anniversary of the formation of the FA. On 21 October they played a 'Rest of Europe' 11 at Wembley, a team containing none of the Hungarian players they were due to meet just a month later.

Selection of Hungary as England's opponents for that international match in November – a 'friendly' in football parlance – owed a lot to chance. FA secretary Stanley Rous (later Sir Stanley and president of FIFA) had attended the Olympic Games in Helsinki in 1952, and watched Hungary trounce a very competent Sweden 6–0. Ever the opportunist, Rous was quick off the mark. Perhaps he saw in Hungary a side that would feature strongly in the 1954 World Cup (he was right in this) and one against which England's own potential could be measured. The fixture was enthusiastically offered to Sandor Barcs, president of the Hungarian FA, but Barcs was not so sanguine; he would need to clear the match with the unbelievably bureaucratic Communist Party officials in Budapest. The sticking point for many months was Barc's reluctance to give the Central Committee a guarantee that Hungary would defeat England. He told them that no such assurance was possible, football being what it was, but if the fixture were to be approved, he could assure them that Hungary would play 'a very, very good game and it would be a world sensation'. The party apparatchiks eventually relented and in a telephone call to

Stanley Rous, the match was fixed for Wednesday 25 November 1953, at Wembley.

Gusztáv Sebes, the Hungarian coach, attended the 90th-anniversary game that October and watched England's performance against the Rest of Europe very closely. England's proud record of home invincibility against foreign opposition was very nearly lost that day and the game finished 4–4, only because England scored from a penalty in the 92nd minute. What Sebes thought of England's performance is not recorded, but there was little doubt about the seriousness with which he viewed the impending England–Hungary friendly. Returning to Wembley the next day, he spent a long time examining the pitch. Its dimensions were carefully recorded and he tried to assess where the sun would be during the match. He noticed that the ball did not bounce as high as expected from the lush turf and, intrigued by this, asked for an English match ball to take back. Stanley Rous obligingly supplied three. Some accounts have it that five were sent by mail, but this seems unlikely. The Hungarian defender Jeno Buzansky commented more scientifically on the differences between English and Hungarian footballs: the English version was harder and playing it felt 'like kicking a wooden ball'. This statement is difficult to understand as almost all the resilience of a football derives from its inflation pressure, precisely controlled under the regulations. Not until very recently have interior linings been inserted between the bladder and the outer casing to alter the playing 'feel', so where this implicit softness in the Hungarian ball could have come from remains a mystery.

In fairness to both teams, though, deciding which ball to play in that era could be a fraught issue. When Argentina and Uruguay played the first World Cup final in 1930 there was no ruling concerning the choice of ball and both sides insisted on their national model. It was resolved by playing the Argentinian ball first and the Uruguayans' in the second half. Uruguay won 4–2, having been 2–1 behind at half-time, so perhaps the switch did the trick. The problems persisted as late as the 1962 World Cup in Chile. For a time the Chileans' insistence that their ball should be used in all matches caused considerable problems. It was of inferior quality, its surface rapidly deteriorating, and it would peel during normal play. Referees secretly compromised. They would start matches with the Chilean ball and switch at the first opportunity to a superior Swedish product. The plan was very nearly frustrated by the Chilean strategy of impounding the Swedish models in customs, but these difficulties were overcome and the superior ball was adopted. This was fortunate as otherwise the world would not have seen the astonishing swerving free kicks produced by Brazil's Garrincha, feats that would have been impossible without the stable aerodynamics of the Swedish ball. Issues concerning the ball notwithstanding, the Hungarians had prepared well and could now begin serious planning. They widened a pitch at home to match Wembley's dimensions and played against teams set up to mimic English tactics. This is possibly the greatest indictment of the rigidity of England's game; misreading the opposition's tactics can be costly, but Hungary must have been very confident in their assessment of England's approach to be so committed in this part of their strategy. Ten days before they played England they met Sweden again in Budapest. The Swedes had clearly learned from their drubbing in Helsinki the previous year, as the game finished with 2 goals each. Much of their success could be put down to the fact that they kept one player, the Hungarian Nandor Hidegkuti, very quiet by man-marking him throughout – it required two players, a different one for each half of the match. England's rather donnish manager, Walter Winterbottom (later Sir Walter), watched this match, and had been present at the earlier encounter between Sweden and Hungary at the Olympic Games. If he saw anything significant it was to remain submerged in his thinking. Hungary played one more game before Wembley when, breaking their journey to London in Paris, they took on a side from the Renault factory, winning, according to

Hidegkuti, 16–1. This is a marvellous image, rather like Brazil bowling up to Ford's plant in Dagenham, offering the lads from the assembly line a kick-about on the local rec.

The Hungarians chose a central location in London and stayed at the Cumberland Hotel near Marble Arch. Exactly 90 years previously a similar group of earnest footballers had met at the Freemasons Tavern in London to thrash out the game's rules; but at the Cumberland Hotel it would be playing tactics that would be revolutionised. Sandor Barcs, having agreed the fixture with Stanley Rous and patiently negotiated with the Hungarian commissars, attended the tactical briefing led by coach Sebes. He records that it lasted four hours and notes that very little of it made any sense to him. Finally, the team's bus pulled out into the Edgware Road and rumbled off to Wembley.

To most of the 100,000 crowd that Wednesday afternoon, the Hungarians must have seemed like unknowns. They had last visited England in 1936, losing 6–2 to England in a match played at Arsenal's ground. There was no mistaking the fact that new talent had arrived, though, even in the pre-match warm-up. Ferenc Puskas, the inside forward who was to be so influential, and Jozsef Bozsik, the midfielder, volleyed the ball to one another, catching it on the instep before volleying it back. They were able to do this for as many as eight repeats, from over 20 metres. Sadly these images have not survived but there are news-reels that tell the essential story of the game.

The instant captured by Fig. 2.3 is the point where the captains, leading out their teams, are conscious that a photographer is shaping up for a picture. Billy Wright, holding the match ball, reacts immediately. He smiles, chin up, and strides forward confidently; Puskas, Hungary's captain, has a rather firmer set to his expression. He walks with more of a swagger and not a little of a roll. Because of his army rank (many of the Hungarians were, at least nominally, serving with the Hungarian military) the press dubbed him 'the Galloping Major'. Although, under the conventions of W-M, Wright would be expected to mark

Fig. 2.3: Hungary and England, 1953

Puskas, ironically this photographic pose would be about as close as he would manage to get to his wily opponent all afternoon. Gil Merrick, the Birmingham City goalkeeper, follows Wright and Gyula Grosics, Merrick's opposite number, tracks Puskas. Grosics stares at the match ball; perhaps he's thinking of Sebes' team talk and trying to assess the likely bounce off the turf. Third in line for Hungary is Hidegkuti, the player who will do most of the damage. He looks down, not dejectedly or overawed but like someone pondering a deeply technical mathematical problem.

The teams' strip is also revealing. England played in traditional white, the Hungarians in red. Recent research has suggested that red confers a distinct advantage in team and individual competition, but this was not known in the 1950s and, as events would show, Hungary needed no such accidental help. It is the regularity of England's turn-out that is striking. The players, even the goalkeeper, sport rolled-up shirt sleeves: not casual, random roll-ups but regulation turns just above the elbow, suggesting an attitude of 'let's get on with the job.' Perhaps they were all inspected before leaving the dressing room. They are wearing the baggy shorts which match programmes of that era still described as 'knickers'. Hungary's look is altogether modern. They have jerseys, emphatically not shirts, with rolled-down sleeves. Their collars are tied up with a lace; England's, although open in the traditionally accepted sense, look starched and could have been buttoned up to take a tie. Billy Wright, glancing at the Hungarians' boots, strangely cutaway around the ankles, memorably summed up England's complacency. Turning, he called over his shoulder to Stan Mortensen, centre forward for Blackpool in that memorable final just six months previously, 'We should be all right, Stan. They haven't got the proper kit.'

Less than a minute after kick-off, Hungary scored. The newsreel record shows Hidegkuti drifting forward and hovering just outside the English penalty area. There is no marker, and he simply waits. The ball is worked to the right, and then played back across midfield. There is a decoy run by Sandor Kocsis, Puskas' fellow striker, across the edge of England's box and then Bozsik slips the ball to the hovering Hidegkuti. He gets away quickly enough now, leaves two defenders for dead and moves into the penalty area. One more touch then a ferocious shot and Merrick is beaten to his right. It was often said by the football pundits that continental opposition couldn't really shoot, but the myth was firmly nailed by the Hungarians that day.

The great problem for England was that Hungary were not playing according to the accepted conventions. Hidegkuti played not as a classical centre forward but in what came to be called a 'deep-lying' position in a midfield partnership with his more defence-minded team mate, Bozsik. The formation was the precursor of 4-2-4, with Hidegkuti and Bozsik playing the demanding roles of central link men. Given that Hidegkuti often went as deep as his own penalty area to pick up the ball, England's centre half, Harry Johnston, was in a quandary. It had been so much easier at Wembley six months previously when Johnston, Blackpool's centre half, had marked Nat Lofthouse who, compared with Hidegkuti, played with absolute predictability. Stay back and Hidegkuti was a free agent in midfield. Follow Hidegkuti and there would have been an enormous hole in central defence, easily exploited by the rampant Hungarian forwards who were now exchanging positions with baffling fluency. The English full backs faced the same problem. Their Hungarian wing opponents were not the conventional product. Sometimes they too went deeper, towards their own goal, to find the ball, and often defended by tracking back with the opposing winger to relieve pressure on their defence. What of Johnston's Blackpool team mate, Matthews? He had moments, but was a shadow of the player who had turned the Cup Final. He was simply denied service as the winger Zoltan Czibor and the back Mihaly Lantos closed him down. Attacks by Hungary often ended with equal numbers of England defenders and Hungarian attackers in the English penalty area, a catastrophic position for defenders. And so the goals for Hungary mounted.

Billy Wright would often cheerfully describe how he was utterly bamboozled by Puskas' first goal. The Hungarian, nominally the inside left, had popped up on the right and worked his way to the corner of the 6-yard (5.5 metres) area. As Wright ran in, Puskas coolly rolled the ball out of the path of his desperate lunge and, with Wright dumped on his backside, hammered the ball home. Puskas was credited with a second goal later in the match, a deflection from Bozsik's free kick. Whether he intentionally played the ball or not is immaterial; England faced up without a defensive wall, presumably because no one was expected to convert a free kick from 30 yards (27 metres). Hungary's fifth goal is especially revealing. Bozsik had chased a ball almost to England's right corner flag. As the move built, Alf Ramsey, England's right full back standing on the far post, threw his arms wide in a gesture of despair. Yet another attack! The ball was passed to Puskas, who cheekily chipped it across the 6-yard box as Bozsik recovered his position in midfield. The Hungarian header was pushed on to the post by keeper Merrick, and in the scrambled clearance the ball was returned to Bozsik, by now well outside the penalty area. He collected, ran forward and beat Merrick yet again with an unstoppable shot. At first it seemed as though the England defence, pushing out, had caught Puskas off-side. But Ramsey, reverting to the only instinct of a full back under extreme pressure, had stayed rigid on the goal line by the far post. As he collected the ball from the net his dejection was obvious and in the distance the camera picked up the lonely figure of Matthews, waiting in the classic English winger's position, for the ball that never came.

England scored three against Hungary's six, an indication that all was not quite right with the Hungarian defence. They were not yet playing what we would call a flat back four, but the left half, Jozsef Zakarias, often worked alongside the conventional centre half, Gyula Lorant, as a second central defender. Ramsey had some consolation: he scored a penalty in the 57th minute, but this time it was a token, not to be compared with his face-saving penalty against the Rest of Europe a month earlier. The only surprising aspect of the result was that Hungary had not scored more. Watching injured in the stand was Tom Finney (Sir Tom in 1998), a winger almost as revered as Matthews for his skilful play, who summed the match up. It was, he said, 'like cart-horses playing race-horses'.

There were some strange footnotes to the game. The following day Stanley Rous met Gusztáv Sebes at the Cumberland Hotel. Perhaps he took a cab from the FA headquarters, then at Cumberland Gate and only a short drive to Marble Arch. He had brought a suitcase which he most likely carried into the hotel himself when the cab drew up. An astonished Sebes was shown the contents of the case. Inside were the Wembley takings for the game. Rous apparently asked how much the Hungarians would like for their share of such a wonderful match. This story seems a touch unlikely, but it was authenticated by the radio commentator Georges Szepesi and by Sandor Barcs. Just how the takings for the previous day could be commuted so quickly the next day to a suitcase full of banknotes is mysterious, but it is a colourful tale. Sebes refused any payment at all, citing Hungary's amateur status, and simply requested a return match in Budapest. This was accepted and scheduled for the following May, presumably now with little opposition from the party officials.

There was a post-mortem of sorts not long after the Wembley débâcle, arranged by the FA and held at the Café Royal in London, involving managers of the top English clubs. They discussed how to deal with such tactics and the threat of players like Hidegkuti. Some favoured the centre half following the deeplying centre forward, others the status quo. If there had been any incisive thinking about countering Hungary's system it would probably have come to nothing anyway. Walter Winterbottom afterwards described how the team at that time was selected. A committee of nine (eight selectors and a chairman with the casting vote) met officially and nominations would be put forward for each playing position. Let us say there were five hopefuls for goalkeeper. Discussion would whittle this down to two and the matter would be put to the vote among the eight selectors. A simple majority would decide, but in the event of a tie, the decision went to the chairman. There is a waspish English joke that the definition of a camel is 'a race-horse designed by a committee'. To paraphrase Tom Finney, it is remarkable that a committee setting out to design a race-horse should have got away so often with a cart-horse, when the outcome could well have been the more ungainly beast.

The team travelled to Hungary for the return game, played on 23 May 1954. This was now World Cup year and England had qualified for the tournament. They must have been aware of the importance of preparation and the need to set the team up both physically and psychologically. There were seven team changes for England: both full backs went, the centre half and four forwards. Hungary made only one change. The game was worse by many orders of magnitude for England and they received an absolute drubbing, 7–1. The Hungarians would comment afterwards on their surprise at England's predictability. The team's personnel had changed greatly but they still played the old, predictable system. It would take more than a decade for new tactical creativity to develop. Alf Ramsey, the full back who had spent that November afternoon in 1953 chasing shadows, would be the unlikely iconoclast, ultimately vindicated in his World Cup triumph at Wembley in 1966. Significantly his condition for taking the manager's job was that he alone should select the side, and out went the cumbrous committee, its endless debates and fatuous votes.

If 4-2-4 had almost arrived it had a little way to go before the world would see the finished article. Hungary, though, went to the World Cup competition in Switzerland in 1954 as strong favourites. Their passage through the group rounds was smooth; on the way they beat West Germany 8–3 and scored 17 goals overall, conceding only three in their qualifying matches. The West Germans, for whom that defeat would not prevent their qualifying for the next stage, were probably biding their time. Their manager, Sepp Herberger, as so often with the great German World Cup sides, was inspirational, a quality that would be needed in the final itself.

Hungary drew Brazil in the quarter-finals, a team that also headed its group, but not so convincingly. The game between the two sides would become notorious as the 'Battle of Berne'. At that time Brazil played with a stopper centre half in a traditional W-M like England, and were open to the guile of a team set up to exploit its weaknesses as ruthlessly as Hungary.

English referee Arthur Ellis was given great credit for bringing the match to any kind of a conclusion that day, as it quickly turned into a violent, ill-tempered affair, with three players sent off. Bozsic exchanged blows with the Brazilian full back Nilton Santos and both were dismissed. Humberto Tozzi, the Brazilian inside forward, aimed a wild kick at a defender and quickly followed. Worse was to come. The Brazilians, beaten 4–2, invaded the Hungarian dressing room and a vicious brawl ensued. Boots and bottles were thrown. In an incident still only partly understood, Puskas, who had not played because of injury, was alleged to have struck the Brazilian centre half with a bottle, causing a severe facial wound. An official of the World Cup Committee apparently witnessed the attack, but in later reports a 'spectator' was said to have been responsible. FIFA pusillanimously delegated action to the individual Brazilian and Hungarian Associations, who took no disciplinary action at all.

The final itself held the ultimate shock for Hungary. Their dream of being World Champions was destroyed by a proficient West Germany, who ran out 3–2 winners. Herberger's managerial talents were exercised to the full after the Germans conceded two early goals. That, against a team with the power and pedigree of Hungary, should really have been 'game over', but defeat was never part of Herberger's vision. It was a match in which Puskas, still hampered by injury, should perhaps not have played, but his influence on the team and his views on who should and should not play were too strong for even Sebes to countermand.

Following the 1954 World Cup both Brazil and Hungary were at a watershed. The Hungarians would never reach such heights again once the heart was ripped out of the team by the Hungarian Uprising in 1956. In that year the authorities had sanctioned a foreign tour by Honved, the club containing the cream of the national side. They were returning to Europe from South America when news came of the Russian invasion of Hungary and the cruel suppression of the uprising. Bozsic and Hidegkuti went back to Hungary, but Puskas, Kocsis and Czibor chose exile. The team Hungary sent to Sweden for the 1958 World Cup was simply not good enough to progress beyond the group stages; not so Brazil, the eventual winners, who, unlike England, had learned from their Hungarian experiences.

Brazil in 1954 must have taken home deep reservations about their game. When it re-emerged in Sweden in 1958 it was emphatically 4-2-4, the finished article and the *de facto* formation standard that all would try to emulate when the competition had run its course. There were suggestions that the formation was a Brazilian innovation introduced by a Paraguayan coach at the Flamengo Club in Rio. If true, this must have been post-1956, as doubts about Brazil's tactics were still being expressed following their uninspiring tour of Europe that year. Some assert that 4-2-4 came straight from a Hungarian source when Bela Guttman, a Hungarian coach fleeing from the 1956 uprising, introduced it to the Brazilians. Whatever its origins, by 1958 the system had been mastered and Brazil had players who were completely attuned to its demands. Their historic set-up is shown in Fig. 2.4.

Four defenders were played in a tight line, a 'flat back four' in today's convention. W-M's inherent weakness was resolved as there was now no need for the defence to pivot around the centre half in response to a threat from the wings. Consequently the full backs in 4-2-4 were less prone to being caught out of position if the point of the attack were switched. Offside could be controlled, and played to advantage, provided that the back four retained their shape and moved as a unit. The defence comprised

Fig. 2.4: Brazil's 4-2-4. World Cup final against Sweden, 1958

two central defenders – there was now technically no centre half – and two full backs. As a flat line is technically vulnerable to a ball played through or over the defence, the central defenders needed to be very mobile and good readers of the game so that they could cover for one another in such cases. The formation also placed greater demands on the goalie, who had to be off his line very quickly if the back four were beaten in this way, and on many occasions it was the keeper who kicked the ball clear from outside his penalty area. Nor were the full backs simply defenders in the classic mould, sitting back marking the opposing winger and hoofing optimistic balls forward; they were now expected to be almost as fast and skilled as wingers, making deep, overlapping runs into the opponents' half.

The engine of the system lay in midfield, where a large burden was shouldered by just two individuals. They were the link men, dedicated to the role of bridging defence and attack and much more versatile than any midfield predecessor. They would double as defenders in a six-man system when their defence was pressured and equally become surrogate forwards when their own attack was dominant. The four forwards tended to play as central strikers and wingers still but, as Hungary had shown, all would be expected to play competently right across the forward line. If the new incarnation of full back behaved occasionally like a winger, then the nominal wingers would defend more, coming back to win the ball, or helping a struggling full back. Brazil were fortunate in 1958 in finding or adapting players to these key roles. Didi and Zito were a perfect match in midfield; the full backs, Djalma Santos especially, overlapped fluently; and in the forward line Pelé and Garrincha ran riot. Brazil deservedly beat Sweden 5–2 in a breathtaking final played in a spirit that expunged the bitter memories of Berne.

By the 1962 World Cup in Chile the formation mutated once again. A weakness of 4-2-4 lay in the demands it placed on the two midfielders; even the most gifted players could be overrun, and playing four forwards under those circumstances was a dangerous luxury. The age-old formula of depleting the forward line was used once more and a third player joined the midfield to create the 4-3-3 formation. Brazil played 4-3-3 and retained their crown that year, beating Czechoslovakia 3–1, but in a final that had none of the brio of the 1958 contest. While Brazil were probably first to play this formation on the world stage, they were not unique in conceiving it. Others had also been experimenting and Alf Ramsey (to become Sir Alf in 1967), who had become a successful club manager, worked a miracle at the relatively unknown Ipswich Town. Joining them in 1955 he took them from the obscurity of the Third Division to the English League Championship in just seven seasons. He too had seen the possibilities of 4-3-3 when he withdrew a traditional winger to play in this deeper role in his Ipswich side. His World Cup-winning team, dubbed the 'wingless wonders', remained faithful to 4-3-3 (Fig. 2.5), beating West Germany 4–2, although in truth the victory had as much to do with the old-fashioned English virtues of hard running and stamina when the teams struggled to break the deadlock in extra time.

Fig. 2.5: England's 4-3-3. World Cup final against West Germany, 1966

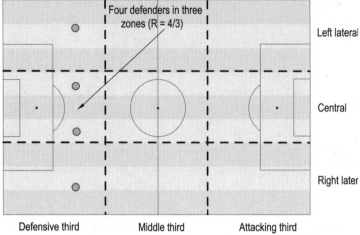

Fig. 2.6: The 9 key zones for defensive, attacking and midfield play.
Attacking side moves left to right

Nowadays there are few teams playing 4-2-4 in the top flight and none following W-M in its traditional format. The systems that succeeded these often seem bewildering in their number and complexity, but teams play in defined formations for a purpose. To see why, we can look at the pitch as a kind of tactical map by dividing it into 9 equal zones in length and width, as shown in Fig. 2.6. The terms 'defensive third', 'middle third' and 'attacking third' in this diagram have obvious connotations as most of the actions concerned with defensive, midfield and attacking strategy take place in these zones. The central and lateral divisions are equally important. Defenders *must* control the vital central region in the attacking third and neutralise threats originating in either of the laterals in this zone. Many goals are scored from assists following defensive mistakes in the attacking laterals.

The objective of any playing formation is to gain possession of the ball and use it productively to score goals. Not surprisingly it is possession gained in the attacking third that is crucial. An important finding of match performance analysis can be quoted to support this. Table 2.1 shows the percentage of goals scored from possessions initially gained in the attacking, middle and defending thirds of the pitch.

Table 2.1: Percentage of goals scored from possessions gained in various zones of the pitch (after Bate)

Areas of pitch	Possessions gained %	Goals scored %
Attacking third	13	66
Middle third	46	26
Defensive third	41	8

This data was collected from 16 international matches and reported by Richard Bate in 1988. Possession won in the attacking third is only 13 per cent of the total, but this produces 66 per cent of all goals scored. Any team looking to win must have this as a prime objective, but not at the expense of surrendering control in the defending and middle thirds. The key questions for any playing system are therefore:

- How well do players cover and control the various zones?
- How efficient is the formation in delivering passes into the attacking third?

We can explore these questions in relation to the most commonly accepted formations in the modern game. Figs. 2.7 a–d show a representative group, but it is by no means exhaustive. The 4-2-4 is included, notwithstanding the comments above, because of its historical impact. It is important to state that the formations indicate where defenders, midfielders and attackers principally operate, but these patterns would, emphatically, not be rigidly followed on the pitch and the formations may only be discernible literally at key points, such as kick-offs or when defenders mark up to face a goal kick. Nevertheless, a formation

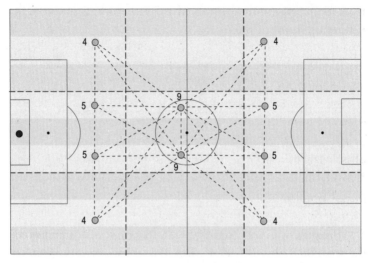

*Fig. 2.7a: Passing options up to 40 metres' length in the 4-2-4 formation.
The numbers show the passes open to each player. There are 54 passes in
total in this formation*

such as 4-2-4 is so described because four defenders cover the defensive third, two midfielders the middle third and four strikers or forwards the attacking third. There would be considerable movement within and between the various zones and, as is well known, defenders often support the attack while attackers sometimes defend deep within their own half of the field when the team is under pressure.

If we were to begin with the 10 outfield players and allocate them to the zones of Fig 2.6, the naïve approach would be to place one in each zone, leaving one spare, who could double up in whatever zone took our fancy. There is a more intelligent way, however, as the historical development of the game has shown. Recognising the importance of defence, we might start by covering the defensive third with a back four, one player for each of the defensive laterals and two guarding the dangerous central zone in front of the penalty area. This is an example of 'redundancy', where more resource is allocated than is strictly required in satisfying the basic objective of one defender per zone. A back four has a redundancy factor R of 4/3 (= four defenders, three zones). Even greater redundancy (R = 5/3) could be achieved by adding a further defender. This is conventionally done using a sweeper. The next issue is how to allocate the remaining six players, or five if a sweeper is used. This depends on how attacking or defensive you wish to be. In the classic 4-2-4 the midfield and attacking redundancies are 2/3 and 4/3 respectively. This is fine if the midfielders can control things, but a midfield with this zonal coverage is dangerously 'pinched' and liable to be swamped if more bodies are pitted against them in the middle third. Just as the formations themselves are not rigidly fixed at each instant of the play, so these attacking and defensive redundancies change as teams gain or lose the advantage throughout the course of the game. A moment's thought reveals that the most flexible way of enhancing defence or attack is by moving midfield players fluidly up and down in support of each. The easiest way of achieving this is to have a formation with players to spare in midfield. Depleting the forward line has been the historical way of achieving this, starting with formations of eight or nine forwards in the 1860s to the frequent use of a lone striker, following much experiment, a century later.

So much for the coverage and control of space, but how efficiently can the ball be moved to the attacking third, our second important criterion for any playing formation? This depends on how efficiently the ball can be passed around from player to player, and not all such passes will end up in the attacking third. Some will go forward when the team is attacking, some backwards, and a number will involve inter-passing between defenders, midfielders and attackers in their respective zones.

Let us look at the standard 4-3-3 of Fig. 2.7 b as an example. To work out the number of passing options for each outfield player in the formation we simply count how many team mates there are within a given radius, say 40 metres, and assume all passes are equally likely within this range. A figure of 40 metres has been chosen as a maximum because the further the ball is hit, the more

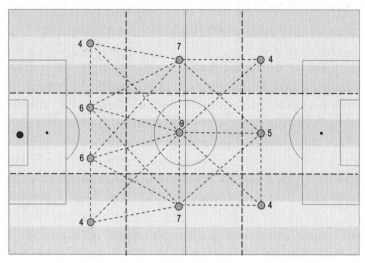

Fig. 2.7b: Passing options in a 4-3-3. There are 56 passes in total

likely it is to be intercepted by a defender. Longer passes can open up defences spectacularly but much above this distance the completion rate (the chance that the ball will reach its target and be

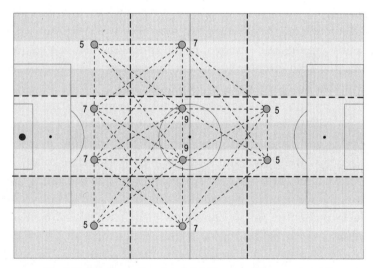

Fig. 2.7c: Passing options in a 4-4-2. There are 66 passes in total

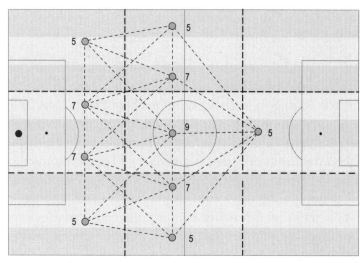

Fig. 2.7d: Passing options in a 4-5-1. There are 62 passes in total

controlled successfully) drops off rapidly. Given these assumptions, there are 56 possible passing sequences in a classic 4-3-3. The numbers for each player in the various formations are shown in the diagrams. These sequences will be continuously cycled in a real game, where there may be in excess of 650 passes by both sides. Only 7 of the possible 56 passes in a 4-3-3, 13 per cent of the total, involve forward passes between midfield and the crucial attacking third. Accepting this figure as a measure of the attacking potential, we can compare the other formations in Table 2.2.

Table 2.2: Passing performance and midfielder workload in standard playing formations

Formation	Total passes under 40 metres	Passes from midfield to attack (%)	Passing load per midfielder (%)
4-2-4	54	15	17
4-3-3	56	13	14
4-4-2	66	12	12
4-5-1	62	8	11

The 4-2-4 with 15 per cent of all passes reaching the attacking third is clearly best while the 4-5-1 (8 per cent) is easily seen to be the most negative formation in this respect. Teams playing this latter set-up have a packed midfield and a lone striker and are usually looking to protect a lead or secure an advantageous draw. Table 2.2 also gives the maximum number of passes possible in each playing formation. The 4-4-2 (66 passing sequences) is the best and the 4-2-4 (54 sequences) the worst. In a 4-4-2 each outfield player has more options available, there being on average 6.6 team mates within striking distance. With tight marking this number will be cut down considerably. But it greatly surpasses 4-2-4 in terms of the ability to move the ball around, as this formation starts with only just over 5.4 players, on average, within striking range of a pass.

The midfield is the area where most bottlenecks are potentially likely to occur as all the traffic, in the form of passes between defence and attack, is processed here. In this respect the loading on the midfielders – how much work they get through in receiving and moving the ball around – in each formation is an important issue. This is not the only drain on energy as players also have to run, and not surprisingly perhaps it is the midfielders who run furthest of all. But restricting the argument to passing, this loading is easily assessed by calculating what proportion of all passes (forwards, backwards and player-to-player) is handled in midfield for each formation. The figures are shown in Table 2.2. Obviously the average loading per midfielder depends on how many players are allocated to this role in each formation, but the average of 17 per cent in a 4-2-4 is much more demanding than in a 4-4-2, where the figure is 12 per cent, and further underlines why the former is no longer in favour in football's top flight.

So far we have looked at systems that evolved essentially from the earliest attempts to address the inherent weaknesses of W-M. At least one system had developed in parallel with it and, although much less extensively played, had a significant influence

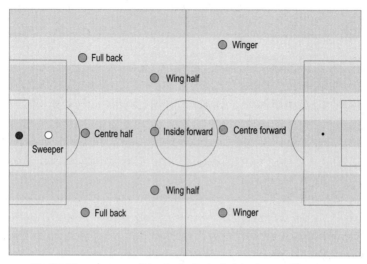

Fig. 2.8: The sweeper position in the 'Swiss bolt' or 'verrou' formation

on attacking and defensive styles from the 1960s onwards. The original system (Fig. 2.8) was developed by the Swiss team coach Karl Rappan in the 1930s and 40s and was known as the '*verrou*', the French word for a door-bolt. The descriptor was apt as the formation relied on a deep-lying defender (later called the sweeper) playing behind the traditional centre half and full backs, effectively slamming the defensive door on any attacker who breached the last line of defenders. The formation, by virtue of moving an attacker to play in this deep position, was more defensive than W-M but not obsessively so.

Its transformation into the most negative system of all is credited to Helenio Herrera, who played it to great effect with his Inter Milan team of the 1960s, but to the detriment of football as a spectator sport. In Italian, the word '*verrou*' becomes '*catenaccio*' in literal translation, and in its football context it means a formation not just bolted, but barred, padlocked and boarded up at every conceivable point of entry. As shown in Fig. 2.9 the sweeper played in the expected position but behind a back four who were assigned absolutely rigid man-marking responsibilities

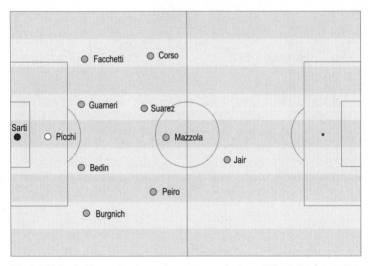

Fig. 2.9: Helenio Herrera's adaptation, catenaccio. *Inter Milan's European Cup winning side, 1965*

against the opposing team's forwards. The midfield players stifled space in front of this defensive shield and the (frequently lone) striker's role was very often simply a token one as the formation rarely pressed into the attacking third. The break-out mechanism involved the overlapping full back, a role perfected by Giacinto Facchetti for both Inter Milan and the Italian national side. It was a formation designed, above all else, to avoid losing games, which is to say that spectators often saw a 1–0 win or an expedient draw ground out through 90 minutes of infinitely tedious play. What is surprising is that the Italian national team, the marvellously gifted 'Azzurri', should have regressed to this depressing formation and that it should have spread so virulently through the Italian senior game in the 1960s. Herrera would protest, in the teeth of all the later criticism, that his system had been traduced and that by using attacking full backs it was not really negative at all. Fortunately, *catenaccio* seems to have disappeared from the modern game. Unless, like the smallpox virus, supposedly isolated from the world's natural environment, it lies deep-frozen in some obscure footballing laboratory, plotting a comeback.

Catenaccio's antithesis, Total Football, made its welcome appearance in the magnificent Dutch and German sides of the 1970s. The term was coined by the media and caught on because it so perfectly described the new spirit of the game and the versatility of the players who made it work. The German model interestingly had the same root as *catenaccio*, but was based on a sweeper increasingly called the *libero*, as he was given free rein to exploit the attacking potential of the role. Within this model the sweeper played in front of the back four in a consciously creative role. Its architect was Franz Beckenbauer, a player said to have been inspired by Facchetti's attacking over-laps in the despised *catenaccio* formation. How much more effective might the tactic be if the surging runs came not from a full back but from a gifted playmaker, raiding from central defence? It posed, in the inverse, the same problem that England had faced and failed to solve against Hungary: an elusive defender coming forward rather than an attacker playing deep. Beckenbauer exploited the possibilities to the full.

The Dutch international side's realisation of Total Football was perhaps more true to the phrase. The attacking and defensive principles were absolutely sound but players' individual roles were subsumed into the game's changing demands, moment by moment. All could play in attack or defend as the need arose. It had brought the Dutch team Ajax, coached by the enormously influential Rinus Michels, three successive European Cups between 1971 and 1973 and seemed tailored for the gifts of Johan Cruyff, the side's star player. Sometimes the question 'Would Team A have beaten Team B?' can be answered only speculatively, but at the 1974 World Cup final the answer was decisive. West Germany, the hosts, beat the gifted Dutch 2–1, in a match billed as the 'Beckenbauer–Cruyff decider'. The Dutch, after a whirlwind opening and an early penalty, were perhaps too arrogant and paid the price. They lost again to the host nation in Argentina at the World Cup four years later, this time fielding a side in which Cruyff had elected not to play.

There are many variations on the basic themes of football tactics and formations. One popular modern option is 3-5-2. Its rationale is that often teams fielding two strikers in a 4-4-2 do not really create many problems for a strong, opposing back four. So the 'spare' defender, usually a full back, can be pushed forward to make 5 in midfield to improve the attacking options. And this principle can be followed during the tactical twists and turns of any game. For example, a team nominally playing 4-4-2 may need to look for a winning goal or an equaliser as the clock runs down. Fine: this time push a midfielder forward and play as a 4-3-3. Or, if you want to be really adventurous, play 4-2-4, which has the greatest attacking potential of all. But be prepared to run out of steam in midfield, and if you get your goal and want to sit on your lead play 4-5-1. All things considered it is not surprising that 4-4-2 has come to be looked upon as almost a universal template, a dependable system for most occasions and a good jumping-off point for tactical development. It has good redundancy (4/3) in the defending and middle thirds, and a glance at Table 2.2 shows that it is very rich in passing options. It also delivers a reasonable proportion of all possession to the important attacking third. If it occasionally varies from the standard pattern, it does so by playing the four midfielders in the so-called 'diamond' formation, where the central midfielders adopt more clearly defined attacking and defensive roles. The defender, the 'holding' midfielder, plays in front of the back four while his colleague plays forward, just behind the strikers in a more attacking role.

Is any system clearly superior to any other? The question is easy to answer when any of the modern formations that displaced W-M is pitted against the historic predecessors. But what if you could clone 22 players of identical ability and play 4-4-2 with one team against 4-3-3 with the other? The answer is not so obvious then and it is not even clear that each of these highly artificial teams, playing *identical* systems, would end up locked in stalemate. Much depends on the degree to which football is influenced by statistical chance. Perhaps, in the final analysis, it is the players who make the system, not the opposite.

CHAPTER 3

ALL IN A SPIN – THE UNSTOPPABLE FREE KICK

The revolution in tactics and playing formations that swept through team football in the 1950s was mirrored by the development of individual playing skills. One of the most important remains the ability to make the ball swerve in flight, very much a South American speciality in the early evolution of this technique. The skill is most often used in direct free kicks, especially from the dangerous frontal positions around the edge of the penalty area, although spin is increasingly being applied in shots at goal in open play. Elite performers are also extending their shooting range, and successful free kicks beyond 30 yards (27 metres) are increasingly frequent. So effortless does the performance seem that fans' expectations have been raised to unrealistic levels. A direct free kick or a penalty; what's the difference when top players can do such magical things with the ball? Of course it was not always like this and the problem for strikers for many years was what to do to beat the defensive wall, introduced precisely to frustrate direct scoring opportunities.

It is not known with certainty how the defensive wall evolved, but its introduction was inevitable after free kicks began to be awarded for handling offences in 1873. The rule was broadened to cover other infringements and by 1902, when pitch markings had settled pretty well into their present format, direct free kicks

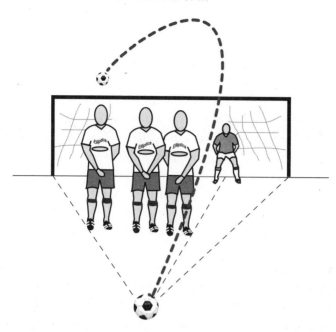

Fig. 3.1: Defensive wall set-up. Wall covers far post and up to 75 per cent of goal line. Goalkeeper lines up with near edge of wall

just outside the penalty area were posing severe problems for defences. A free shot from this distance had to be nullified. If defenders were forced to stand 10 yards (9.1 metres) from the kick, so be it; but they could still legally form up in a tightly positioned 'wall' at this distance, blocking the line for a direct shot (Fig. 3.1). There is considerable variation in the number of players needed in the wall depending on the angle of the kick and the distance from goal. In its most conventional form the wall is set up so that the defenders cover the far post and about 75 per cent of the goal line. The goalkeeper lines up with the near edge of the wall, leaving him, in theory at least, a clear view of the shot.

For many years the tactic was simply to blast the ball at the wall, hoping that the defenders would separate, leaving a gap; or perhaps there would be a fortuitous deflection, sending the ball beyond the keeper. If the wall had been correctly set up and defenders kept their heads, all would be well, but it took real courage to stand there in the days when a waterlogged, muddy lump of leather was belted at you at 30 metres per second (67 mph).

From the striker's point of view, practically the only way to beat a well-positioned wall in the early days, short of the 'hit and hope approach', was to play a shot that *just* cleared the heads of the defenders. This needed very fine judgement and frequently the outcome was a shot that also cleared the bar. Too much velocity is a problem and, as we shall see, so is the wrong kicking action. Any tendency to get the foot *under* the ball creates backspin that makes it rise. Keeping the ball speed down is possible using a softer, chip-type shot, but this seldom causes problems for an alert goalkeeper. In Italy today, special contempt is reserved for any keeper beaten in this way; the shot is called '*il cucchiaio*', 'the spoon', because of the exaggerated scooping, stabbing action used in kicking the ball.

The problem is that gravity and air resistance, the forces that tend to bring the ball down in a conventional shot, need a finite distance in which to operate to do their job effectively. Any element of backspin militates against this, especially for typical free kick distances of 20–25 yards (18–23 metres). What is needed is a technique that allows the ball to be struck at a rapid pace, above about 25 metres per second, while avoiding the damaging effects of backspin. If it can also be swerved beyond the goalkeeper's reach, so much the better.

The vital ingredient in achieving all this is an action that produces sidespin, and the first player to exploit it was the magnificent Brazilian midfielder 'Didi', Waldir Pereira. He might never have played at all. At 14 years of age he faced the very real possibility of leg amputation because of a badly infected knee. Fortunately he made a complete recovery and went on to play with great distinction for Brazil in the 1954, 1958 and 1962 World Cup competitions. It was, in fact, one of his free kick 'specials' that gave Brazil a narrow 1–0 victory over Peru and ensured their qualification for the 1958 tournament in Sweden. Astonishingly his selection was in doubt right up to the first game, and there had been talk of his not being chosen for the competition at all. He drily quipped that to leave him out would have been uncharitable; his free kick had, after all, paid for the team's ticket to Sweden.

Intriguing reports on Didi's technique emerged in the middle 1950s when Brazilian fans and the media began to use the expression '*folha seca*' to describe his free kicks. This means literally 'dry leaf' in Portuguese but the term was freely translated as 'falling leaf' in the English media. Didi evidently made the ball drift in the air just as a leaf does when it spins and falls to earth; many people were convinced that the ball also 'faded', that is, deflected exaggeratedly in mid-air towards the end of its flight, an observation that still causes controversial debate when free kicks are studied or reported today. What no one disputes, however, is that a ball struck hard enough with sidespin will follow a curling trajectory. In any case the rather poetic 'falling leaf' soon gave way to the more prosaic term 'banana ball', as Didi's methods began to be emulated by European players. This term is no longer fashionable and 'swerve' or 'curl' seem to be the order of the day.

Didi, who can truly be called the inventor of the swerving free kick, practised his technique exhaustively, as do most of today's elite performers such as David Beckham and Zinedine Zidane. His free kicks in the 1958 and 1962 World Cups, in Sweden and Chile respectively, were legendary. He swerved the ball by striking it with the outside of his right foot, a technique called '*os tres dedos*' or 'three toes' in Brazilian parlance. This action can produce considerable sidespin but, compared with instep kicking, makes elevation and direction more difficult to control. Sadly there are few surviving images on film that enable us to analyse Didi's specific technique, but there is no doubt that spectacular kicks of this kind have generally come off when players have swerved the ball around the wall rather than over it. Who can forget the monstrous swerve placed on the ball in exactly this way by Brazilian Roberto Carlos in the Tournoi de France match in 1997? Fully 35 yards (32 metres) from goal, he hammered the ball with the outside of his left foot; it passed the right-hand edge of the wall before moving sharply back to the left, entering the goal off the post. The bemused French goalkeeper, Fabien Barthez, simply stared, rooted to the spot.

Why the technique had not been exploited earlier and more widely in football is curious. By the 1950s golfers were routinely using deliberate hooks or slices to overcome obstructions. Spin was an important component in tennis, and in baseball the curveball was a standard weapon in pitching. In fact spin *was* used in soccer, but not consciously and not initially in the area of free kicks. Wingers had become very adept at taking in-swinging corners and would often claim that a goal that resulted directly from the kick had been deliberately contrived. To deliver an in-swinger, spin was certainly being applied to the ball but, in Europe at least, few players seem to have exploited this weapon by attempting to 'shape' the ball over the shorter delivery distances of the free kick.

The reason why the technique emerged first in the South American game may simply be that playing conditions were, more often than not, warm and dry. The ball seldom resembled its European counterpart: waterlogged, over-weight and, as a consequence, very unresponsive to the aerodynamic forces produced by ball spin. Surface wetness also makes it difficult to create enough friction between boot and ball to achieve adequate spin in the first place. Not until the modern ball with its synthetic, non-absorbent coating arrived in the 1960s could consistent playing qualities be guaranteed. European players then began to emulate the many South Americans using swerve in both dead-ball and passing movements and who, like Didi earlier, had joined European clubs. The masters were copied slavishly and midfielders began to cultivate the swerving cross-field pass, deliberately swinging the ball around an intervening defender. The pass was usually delivered Didi-fashion with the outside of the foot to demonstrate that the skill had been completely assimilated. It was considered very flash in the English game.

To understand how a skilled free-kicker can swerve a ball so dramatically we need to dig a little into the aerodynamics of ball flight. The underlying theory, fluid dynamics, is a complex science, very much a product of twentieth-century mathematics and almost entirely dependent on the power of modern computers to run the associated software. The first person to unlock the secrets of the flight of a spinning ball worked in the late nineteenth century, however. He was Peter Guthrie Tait (Fig. 3.2), an eminent Scottish scientist and mathematician, who made the break-through by analysing the flight of a golf ball.

Fig. 3.2: Peter Guthrie Tait (1831–1901), Scottish mathematician

In 1848 Tait began his mathematical studies at Cambridge. Perhaps in the winter of that year he walked past the very football match at Trinity College where Etonians were howling at Rugbeians for their uncouth handling and carrying approach to the game. He might have laughed but would not have given the proceedings a second glance. His passion was golf; when later he became Professor of Natural Philosophy at Edinburgh, he and his family would decamp to Aberdeen in the summer recess. There he would frequently play an astonishing five rounds of golf a day over the historic Old Course at St Andrews. He was usually deputed to entertain the scientific dignitaries who came to Scotland to attend the often contentious meetings of the British Association for the Advancement of Science. One visitor, the German physicist Helmholtz, was bullied into playing golf. In a letter home, he complained to his wife, 'Mr Tait knows of nothing else here but golfing. (He) is a particular sort of savage; lives here, as he says, only for his muscles, and it was not until today, Sunday, when he dared not play, . . . that he could be brought to talk of rational matters.'

On one occasion Tait proposed a late game in the gathering St Andrews twilight. To make the balls visible he had them coated with phosphorus, not the anodyne paint we use today but the fiery substance that combusts spontaneously on exposure to air. The golfers had just crossed the Swilcan Burn on the Old Course when the inevitable happened. One player picked up a ball and his glove burst into flame. Back at the clubhouse it was 'Darwin's bulldog', the eminent biologist T. H. Huxley, no mean golfer himself, who applied first aid.

It was only natural that Tait would try to apply his science to the game that fascinated him and he kept coming back to a deceptively simple question: why does the ball spend such a relatively long time in the air in a good drive? A 'good drive', given the equipment of the day, meant anything over 180 yards (165 metres) for the range, the distance the ball travelled horizontally before hitting the ground. The corresponding time of flight would be just over 6 seconds. Using simple estimates Tait's calculated value for this number was 3 seconds, much too short and a range over three times the expected value of 180 yards: clearly, with such discrepancies, something was seriously wrong. Tait decided to build a mathematical model of the ball's flight in the hope that, reduced to a fundamental description of the processes, his model would produce new insights into the problem. He had some solid facts to go on. The range should be 180 yards, the time of flight just over 6 seconds and the shape of the trajectory should look like a real golf drive – its highest point should not be half-way, but shifted towards the end of the flight at about 70 per cent of the range.

The first job, though, was data collection. Tait set about this using an extraordinary mixture of informed guesses and precise, if eccentric, experiment. To find the ball's initial velocity, a key parameter in modelling the flight, he used a ballistic pendulum, a fairly conventional device in physics. Imagine the pendulum of a grandfather clock with the weight at the end – the 'bob' – made of some energy-absorbing material. An object whose speed we want to measure is fired into the bob and the pendulum's deflection is proportional to the speed of the incoming object. Tait's specially constructed version was a monster and was mounted so that it could swing freely in a doorway in the basement of his physics lab. The bob was a 1-foot (30-cm) diameter target zone filled with soft clay. The aim was to drive the ball into this, and to achieve it he persuaded some of the best golfers of the day to do their stuff. Momentum transfer did the rest and the initial speed of the ball could be calculated by noting the pendulum's deflection. Very straightforward, except that the person taking the readings was right in the line of fire and had to crouch behind the partially closed door as the ball whistled by his head. Although they hung coconut matting around the door frame there were occasional mishits and we can imagine the scientists diving for cover as the ball went pinging around the laboratory walls.

Even with the most precisely measured inputs a mathematical model is only as good as the sophistication of the physics built into it. At first Tait made the simplest assumption possible, that the ball moved freely under gravity with no air resistance. The flight path was easily calculated and plotted as a graph. The shape was the familiar parabola, but the calculated range, nearly 600 yards (550 metres), was enormous. Not even today's biggest hitters with modern high-tech equipment would achieve this performance. The shape of the trajectory was also wrong, with the vertex half-way down the range.

The next step was to include air resistance. This was well understood in the nineteenth century and, fortunately, various researchers had published tables of the resistive force based on gunnery measurements. Tait was able to scale the data to produce fairly accurate information for the drag on a golf ball. The complexity of the maths increased but this time the range came out nearly 45 yards (41 metres) short of the expected value of 180 yards (165 metres). What was missing was a mechanism intermediate between these extremes, and Tait began to think in terms of a third force that would prolong the flight by counteracting both gravity and drag throughout. His breakthrough came when he remembered a chance remark in Newton's writings in which the great scientist recalled observing how a tennis ball would swerve when it was struck with 'an oblique racket', what we would nowadays call a sliced shot.

Newton was groping towards a theory of light, and imagined it to be composed of microscopically small particles. He wanted to explain optical refraction, the bending of a ray of light when it passes through a prism. Suppose when the ray struck the prism obliquely, the glass surface acted just like a racket face and imparted spin to the particles; presumably they would deflect, just like a tennis ball. Newton was wrong on this occasion but Tait saw the connection instantly. When a golf club with its lofted face strikes the ball it imparts savage backspin. Spin might just be the mechanism that would produce an upward force, countering both gravity and drag throughout the flight. He reasoned that this lift would be present only when the ball was both spinning and moving forward, and his research was almost complete when he found that several investigators had been there before. The first person credited with describing this new force was the German physicist Heinrich Magnus, who in 1852 investigated air flowing over rotating cylinders; the effect now bears his name although it had been studied and reported on in relation to artillery rounds over a century earlier by the English polymath Benjamin Robins. Magnus showed that the lifting force was always perpendicular to the direction of motion and the spin axis. In other words, for a cylinder (or a ball) rotating with backspin the force would be upwards, just as Tait had envisaged.

So far, so good, but mathematically modelling the flight, including the Magnus force, gravity and drag, was immensely more complicated. Even today the equations he derived have not been solved in exact mathematical form and Tait was forced to approximate. He split the whole trajectory into small segments 6 feet (1.8 metres) long and built up the solution step by step. The grinding drudgery of computing the ball's coordinates fell to his laboratory assistant, Mr James Wood, in Tait's description 'an extremely rapid and accurate calculator'. He needed to be: there were many thousands of tedious arithmetical operations, based on frequent references to mathematical tables. Worse, Tait was trying to match his model with the observed trajectory by varying the strength of the Magnus force. This involved starting off with some initial guess and seeing how the eventual trajectory worked out. The long-suffering Mr Wood doubtless set off on many abortive calculations before an acceptable value for the strength of the Magnus force was correctly guessed, but he got there in the end. Today anyone with a simple spreadsheet could replicate Mr Wood's calculations – a chore that took him many months – in a fraction of a second. They would find no mistakes in his manual calculations, a remarkable testimony to his perseverance and accuracy.

Fig. 3.3 shows the results. A ball moving under gravity alone flies too far, but gravity and drag acting together bring the ball to earth too soon; aerodynamic lift was the missing ingredient, essential for a complete explanation of the trajectory including the range, position of vertex and time of flight. There could now be no dispute that a moving, spinning ball would experience a deflecting force. This was the first serious application of science to a sports subject and Tait deserves to be credited with the invention of sports science as a modern discipline.

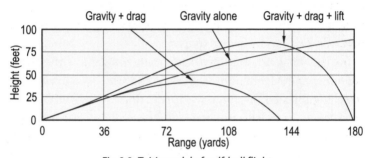

Fig. 3.3: Tait's model of golf-ball flight

Having successfully matched his model to his observations of a driven golf ball, Tait was able to calculate the strength of the force produced by the ball's spin. This turned out to be a little greater than the weight of the ball for a large proportion of the trajectory, and he realised that over most of its flight a golf ball is effectively weightless. Tait was eager to press on, exploring new avenues of his discovery, but we read a plaintive sentence in his scientific paper of 1896. 'Mr Wood,' he writes, 'has gone to Australia.' Whether to recover his sanity or to make his fortune we shall never know.

These results were presented almost at the close of the nineteenth century. Tait published his work in the scientific journals *Nature* and *Transactions of the Royal Society of Edinburgh*, frequently presenting his findings in person to meetings of the latter body.

Golfers were outraged. They believed that the finest driving technique depended on strength and timing and that spin was always detrimental. Now they were being asked to accept that the mechanism responsible for some of the worst shots in golf, namely hooking and slicing, was absolutely fundamental to the art of long driving. Tait, of course, had the last laugh posthumously: an enormous industry has grown up in golf (and other ball games) based on designing specific characteristics into the ball, to increase spin or reduce aerodynamic drag, largely on principles first established by him. He had also unlocked the secret of why any moving, spinning ball will swerve in flight, but it was to be over half a century before Didi independently exploited this when developing his 'folha seca' free kick.

Tait quantified the forces acting on a spinning ball but the science of the day was not sufficiently advanced to explain the aerodynamic effects underlying his observations. Why a football behaves as it does in a free kick is due largely to the physical properties of air and the way it flows around the moving ball. Air is not the substance of many people's imagination. It is relatively dense and exhibits viscosity, or frictional resistance to flow, properties we associate more conventionally with a fluid. Exactly how air flows around the ball's surface, and under some conditions separates from it, is crucial to an understanding of the swerving free kick.

First imagine a non-spinning ball moving forward with air flowing around its surface contours. The problem is that a sphere is not a very efficient aerodynamic shape and only at very low speeds can the air-flow follow the surface intimately. At higher speeds it begins to separate (Fig. 3.4 a). Notice that the smooth, streamlined flow has broken up into a turbulent wake downstream. Turbulence always causes drag, effectively by robbing the moving object of kinetic energy. At higher speeds, flow separation occurs even earlier, the volume of the turbulent wake increases and so does the drag. But at a certain point a strange thing happens (Fig. 3.4 b): the turbulent region begins to encroach

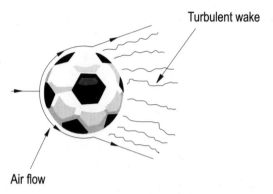

Fig. 3.4 a: Air-flow around slowly moving, non-rotating ball. Flow breaks away early from surface. High associated drag

backwards into a very thin boundary layer in contact with the ball's surface. At this point the flow locks on to the surface once more, the turbulent wake reduces and the drag drops appreciably.

This dramatic reduction in drag force is important in all ball games, football especially. The transition from high to low drag occurs at between 4.5 and 6.7 metres per second (10 and 15 mph) for a football. Since most of the game is played with the ball moving above this speed, almost all the actions such as passing, throwing or shooting are comfortably within the low-drag regime. This is very convenient for elite free-kickers such as David Beckham, whose free kick deliveries are usually between

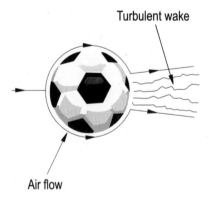

Fig. 3.4 b: Flow around faster-moving ball. Reduced turbulence and drag

27 and 31 metres per second (60 and 70 mph), handsomely above the threshold speed.

The important switch from high to low drag is usually triggered by some form of surface imperfection. The panel stitching on a football, an 'imperfection' of only a millimetre or so deep, is sufficient to do the trick; on golf balls, surface dimples were introduced for exactly the same purpose. It is important to remember that the transition depends on the type of ball – a volley ball, for example, displays different characteristics from a soccer ball – and the trick is to know how to exploit the differences in each game. It is also very counter-intuitive that a ball with a slightly rough surface should have a better performance in terms of aerodynamic drag than a smooth one and quite fortuitous that footballs have always been made with this inbuilt property. Manufacturing perfectly smooth balls would pose no problems at all, but no footballer would tolerate the sluggish, unpredictable behaviour of such an object.

A football, then, can be moved at a brisk pace in a free kick, thanks to boundary layer effects. What happens when it also spins? The detailed flow pattern around a ball revolving with

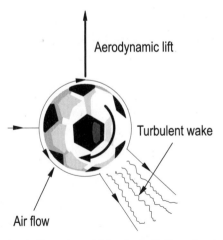

Fig. 3.5: Moving ball rotating with backspin. Deflected wake causes aerodynamic lift

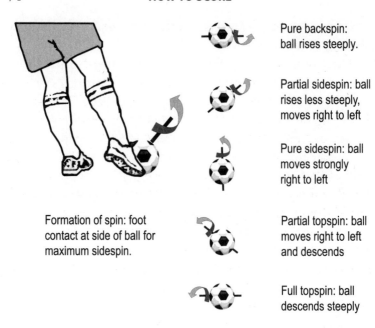

Pure backspin: ball rises steeply.

Partial sidespin: ball rises less steeply, moves right to left

Pure sidespin: ball moves strongly right to left

Formation of spin: foot contact at side of ball for maximum sidespin.

Partial topspin: ball moves right to left and descends

Full topspin: ball descends steeply

Fig. 3.6: Formation of spin axis in free kick

backspin can be seen in Fig. 3.5. The flow is found to separate earlier at the points on the surface rotating against the moving air stream and later on the parts rotating in the same direction as it. As the illustration shows, the turbulent wake is modified, compared with a non-spinning ball, and this asymmetry produces a pressure differential, a deflecting force that gives the ball aerodynamic lift. Detailed measurements show that its direction is indeed always perpendicular to the velocity and the spin axis, as Magnus discovered. If, for example, the ball in Fig. 3.5 rotated with topspin, the sense of the Magnus force would be inverted and the ball would be forced downwards, a property very familiar to tennis players, who deploy it in topspin drives and serves.

Fig. 3.6 shows that by striking the ball progressively more on the side, rather than underneath, the free-kicker produces increasing sidespin. As the spin axis tilts, so does the direction of the Magnus force and it moves progressively from the vertical (backspin) to the horizontal (sidespin). This is exactly the technique invented by Didi, although, as explained, he chose to strike the ball with the outside of the foot rather than with the instep. If the ball can be struck absolutely perfectly on its side, it will spin about a vertical axis; looked at from above, a ball rotating anti-clockwise will move from right to left. The direction flips if the rotation is clockwise. As we have seen, backspin is to be avoided at all costs in free kicks, but a goal-keeper, kicking for distance in a goal kick, attempts to get maximum backspin on the ball to ensure, as in Tait's case, that the Magnus force keeps it in the air as long as possible.

Suppose the ball can be struck so that the spin axis is tilted beyond the vertical, as shown in Fig. 3.6, and topspin is imparted. In this case the Magnus force will have a *downward-pointing* component, meaning that the ball will both swerve and dip. It can also be hit harder than a conventional sidespin kick as the striker can confidently rely on topspin to keep it down. Such free kicks are especially feared by goalkeepers. Not only is the flight less predictable than a sidespin delivery but the increased speed also leaves much less time for the keeper to react in the cru-cial few tenths of a second after the ball clears the defensive wall.

Hitting a stationary ball with topspin from the ground is, of course, exceptionally difficult since there is very little space for the foot to contact the ball with the ascending delivery required in this shot. A very few elite players manage to do this: some idea of the necessary technique can be seen in Fig. 3.7, which gives a good idea of the absolute repeatability of David Beckham's action: the images, taken nearly a year apart, could almost be superimposed. Notice that Beckham is dragging his foot up and over the ball, very much like a topspin drive in tennis. The extreme leaning angle of the body is vital in producing sufficient clearance for the foot to complete this action. Obviously, if the ball could be played in the air there would be much more room for the foot to strike the ball with an unimpeded, ascending delivery. This frequently occurs when players hit the ball on the

Fig. 3.7: Beckham's topspin delivery

volley and topspin is often applied unconsciously in the kicking action. If the shot is on target a goal often results because of the combined speed and dipping flight of the ball. One memorable free kick that exploited this technique ranks with the sidespin effort of Roberto Carlos in 1997 and has passed, like his, into football legend.

On 3 October 1970 Coventry City met reigning League Champions Everton at Highfield Road. With ten minutes remaining, Coventry were awarded a central free kick just outside the penalty area. Willie Carr stood facing Everton's four-man defensive wall, the ball at his feet. Referee Tommy Dawes signalled for the kick, but Carr, instead of moving away from the ball, flicked it with a back-heel action into the air. The Coventry players, who had rehearsed the move, called this 'the donkey kick' for obvious reasons. Waiting to pounce was Ernie Hunt, who ran in and volleyed the ball with the outside of his right foot in a perfect, ascending topspin strike; it flashed over the wall and dipped into the corner of the net. Pandemonium! Referee Dawes thought for a few seconds then awarded the goal. Harry Catterick, Everton's manager, was not impressed and complained that the move was 'Like something out of a circus'.

There has always been a strongly conservative streak in the English game, and football's officialdom, meeting the following season, outlawed the kick. In their pedantic ruling the ball had not travelled a full circumference forwards or backwards before Hunt hit it, and so the move, according to the rules, was illegal. Very little has been seen of this virtually unstoppable and highly entertaining kick since, although a few players have tried to stay within the letter of the law by passing the ball a short distance so that it can then be flicked into the air and hammered goalwards.

Studying simulated free kicks, it is possible to see just how important it is that the delivery of the shot is judged exactly right. Our original research (Bray and Kerwin, 2003) is very much like Tait's in concept. The ball's flight in an experimental kick is captured using fast digital cameras, each arranged to view the trajectory from a different angle. This gives a stereoscopic view, important if the individual images are later to be reconstructed so that true 3-D coordinates can be obtained from the data. First, though, the images are manually digitised at each time step, i.e. for each image frame, on a high-resolution computer monitor. This is about as close as the process gets to Mr Wood's grinding chore, as many thousands of images have to be logged to build up the trajectory. Fortunately, new software packages are emerging that can track the ball and report its coordinates automatically provided the image quality is good. The final stage of the process is again similar to Tait's: a 3-D mathematical model of the ball's flight is compared with the measured coordinates and the aerodynamic variables adjusted in the model until the closest possible fit between theory and experiment is obtained. Unlike Tait though, who was looking for agreement based on only three parameters (range, time of flight and position of vertex), we iterate repeatedly until the model and experimental coordinates agree as closely as possible at *every* measured position. The endpoint of the process is essentially determination of just two numbers: the aerodynamic coefficients that scale the drag and Magnus forces acting on the ball. Once these coefficients are

HOW TO SCORE

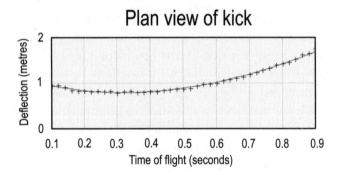

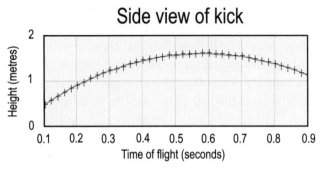

Fig. 3.8: Plan and side views of swerving free kick

found the mathematical model is effectively calibrated and can then be used to simulate free kicks of any type by using various kicking speeds and orientations of the spin axis to replicate sidespin or topspin efforts.

Some idea of the accuracy achieved in the above work can be seen in Fig. 3.8, which shows an example of the best fit between the model and the measured 3-D coordinates of the ball. The crosses on the graphs represent the experimental measurements and show the ball's position at each time step. We were able to locate the ball's position to an accuracy of just over 2 cm in a free kick of 20 metres.

The top graph is effectively a bird's-eye view of the kick and gives some idea of the lateral swerve that can be placed on the ball by a good sidespin kicker. The bottom graph represents a side view as the ball rises over the defensive wall and descends towards the goal. This information was obtained using a human subject to deliver the kicks, but as this can be very gruelling when repeated accuracy is required over a long experimental session, we increasingly use a ball launcher for this type of work. It can be programmed to deliver any kind of 'kick', with any combination of release speed, elevation and ball spin.

It may be helpful in looking at the free kick simulations to keep a few figures in mind. First of all, spin. Fortunately the ball does not need to rotate anything like a golf ball in a free kick – it would not in any case be humanly possible to impart that kind of spin. Rates of several thousand rpm are common in golf, but in free kicks, ball rotation is between about 5 to 10 revolutions per second (300–600 rpm), very slow by comparison. A free kick from around 25 yards (23 metres) from goal takes about one second to reach the goal line, so the ball has time to make only between 5 and 10 complete revolutions during the flight. Spin rates are usually measured from digital images of specially marked balls in the kinds of experiment described above, but manufacturers' own markings, logos and suchlike conveniently enable rotation speed and orientation of the spin axis to be picked out in the many slow-motion replays included in televised games. There is a correlation between spin produced and kicking speed, depending on exactly where the foot strikes the ball. Broadly speaking, speed of delivery is between 60 and 70 mph (27–31 metres per second) and spin rates up to the maximum, around 600 rpm, are achievable. Most free-kickers favour sidespin and produce the lower-speed release to help keep the ball down. The elite performers who can impart some additional topspin usually belt the ball harder and delivery speeds are often slightly above the 70 mph figure.

Fig. 3.9 shows simulated free kicks from a central position 25 yards (23 metres) from goal where the striker, starting from pure backspin, is assumed to apply progressively more sidespin to the shot. A delivery speed of 27 metres per second (60 mph)

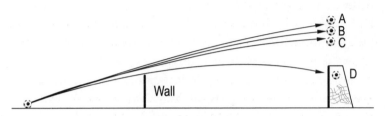

Sidespin free kicks: side view

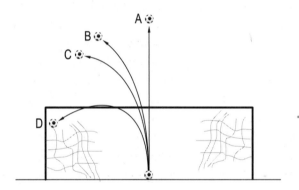

Sidespin free kicks: rear view

A: 0°   B: 30°   C: 45°   D 90°

Fig. 3.9: Effect of increasing sidespin on free kick

has been assumed. The ball is initially struck along the centre line to goal but rapidly deflects from this path depending on the degree of sidespin achieved. Both the side and rear views show the point at which the ball reaches the goal line, whether it misses the target or not.

As noted earlier, practically any component of backspin in the kick is detrimental to hitting the target, as is clearly evident in the figures. The ball played with pure backspin simply skies over the bar and not until the spin axis is almost vertical is it possible to bring the ball down sufficiently to threaten the goal. However, if pure sidespin can be applied there is a further payoff as lateral deflections of around 3.5 yards (3.2 metres) are achievable. Given the classic goalkeeper positioning for this type of kick (cf. Fig. 3.1) the gap for the keeper to close is about 5.5 yards (5 metres), usually too much in the limited time available, first to react to the shot and then to get across to make the save. It is worth recalling how few free kicks are actually *saved* in practice. It is the striker who *misses*, because the shot either fails to hit the target or cannons uselessly into the wall.

The free kicks in Fig. 3.10 show two topspin examples: one is typical of David Beckham's or Zinedine Zidane's action, where the spin axis has been tilted 30 degrees beyond the vertical, usually about as much topspin as can be achieved with an instep delivery kicked from the ground. The other simulates the Carr–Hunt 'donkey kick', played from above the ground where a spin axis 45 degrees beyond vertical has been assumed. This is a fairly modest figure for a ball played on the volley and near-complete topspin could be achieved in a well-contrived kicking action.

Comparison of the sidespin and topspin shots in the figures clearly shows the effectiveness of topspin in keeping the ball down. Lateral deflections are not quite as great as in purely sidespin deliveries but this is amply compensated for by the faster transit time to goal. For example, the Carr–Hunt special would cross the goal line two tenths of a second *earlier* than the scoring sidespin effort of Fig. 3.9. This simply reflects the faster delivery

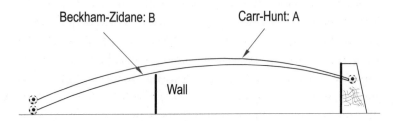

Topspin free kicks: side view

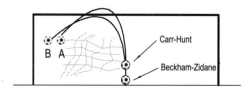

Topspin free kicks: rear view

Fig. 3.10: Effect of increasing topspin on free kick

speed in topspin kicks, but this is the very point of the technique. Two tenths of a second may not seem much but the goalkeeper needs every bit of reaction time available to him when he's struggling to pick up the ball's movements against the background mêlée of players in and around the wall.

Are any of these shots truly unstoppable? The answer must be 'yes', when the execution is perfect, but that's the catch. There is not much margin for error on the striker's part and by running the computer models simulating free kicks of all kinds it is easy to show just how demanding the skill requirements are in practice. Just a degree wrong in the delivery angle of the ball, or a couple of mph overcooked in the shooting speed, and the attempt fails.

In conclusion we can take a look at a couple of instances where spin plays an important part in the outcome but where an unstoppable shot has nothing to do with the intentions of the kicker. These are the frustrating occasions (for the goalkeeper) when the ball picks up spin in a chance deflection, so that a shot

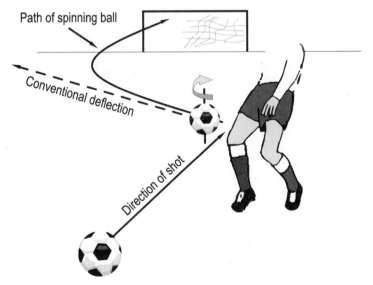

Fig. 3.11: Sidespin deflection

that would have missed the goal by a mile ends up in the net.

Fig. 3.11 shows a ball deflecting off a defender's knee: it could be the leg or thigh, or practically any part of the defender's anatomy the ball hits in a glancing strike. The ball picks up sidespin in the impact and, provided that not too much velocity is lost, begins to move at the expected deflection angle, wide of the net. But the combined velocity and sidespin induce a deflecting force, perversely in the right direction (for the striker), and a goal results. The absolutely galling point for the keeper is that he has almost certainly covered the expected shot, but ends up beaten by an unstoppable fluke. Very much the same thing happens when the ball is deflected vertically after impact with a defender's leg or foot. Topspin is induced and the hapless keeper can only watch as the ball rises over his head then dips steeply into the net.

Could this technique be deliberately exploited? Why not? Who could have imagined more than half a century ago that a young Brazilian would practise his kicking technique obsessively until he could achieve controlled swerve; that three decades ago, two Coventry City players would come up with something as outrageous as their topspin double-act? Or that a young David Beckham would stay on the practice ground long after training had finished so that he could squeeze an element of topspin into his ground shots with such deadly effect? Perhaps there are coaches and professionals out there who are scheming over the possibilities of contrived deflections, to add yet another weapon to the striker's armoury. There is also probably a committee of soccer bureaucrats waiting to slap a prohibition order on whatever they come up with.

CHAPTER 4

MEASUREMENT, MOVEMENT AND FUELLING THE HUMAN ENGINE

After Tait's groundbreaking work on ball flight, the fledgling discipline that would eventually become sports science effectively went to sleep. Read any major review article in today's sport science journals and you will find no citations – references to papers of specific interest or importance – to serious work in sport dated much before the early 1950s. This is not to diminish the enormous contribution made to football by enlightened coaches and players in the intervening period. There would not otherwise have been the radical change in playing systems, the emergence of highly individual playing styles and the mastery of complex skills. Sports scientists were very much in the future, but there were a few signs of change afoot in some international teams' professional approach. When the Brazilians arrived for the 1958 World Cup tournament in Sweden following their traumatic experiences four years before in Switzerland, their team boasted both a doctor and a psychologist. The former had scouted in Sweden the previous year and prepared a lengthy dossier on suitable venues for the team's accommodation and training facilities. Not much is known about the techniques employed by their psychologist but Brazil seemed, in their outlook and in their new playing formation, to have exorcised the demons of Berne. By contrast, England were travelling without a team doctor as late as the 1962 World Cup finals in Chile. They very nearly paid for this lack of foresight following the life-threatening condition suffered during the tour by defender Peter Swan. It was Alf Ramsey, appointed England manager after another World Cup failure in 1962, who repaired this omission.

Sport science's long dormancy came to an end in the 1950s when serious papers again began to appear. There was a growing realisation that sport was as valid a field of study as many of science's more traditional disciplines and, equally important, that athletes could befit from the fruits of scientific research. Football was slower off the mark and it was not until the 1960s that serious attention was turned to the popular game. But from that decade onwards success in football became less hit-and-miss as convention and prejudice were challenged by a battery of quantitative techniques, from the precise measurement of player movements during actual matches to determination of the specific skills used in precision kicking and heading. Absolutely fundamental to all this was the ability to dig below the surface of human perception – the imperfect and often misleading view of the world revealed by our limited faculties – and to record and measure movement in minute detail.

Tait overcame these difficulties using his novel theoretical and practical insights; but suppose that, instead of hammering golf balls into a ballistic pendulum and measuring the tiny deflections, he could have studied high-speed images and obtained velocity and launch angle from a few simple measurements on a permanent record of the event. This was possible in principle using photography, and he would certainly have been aware of the scientific possibilities of the medium. But even with the improvements in photographic technique in the 1870s, conventional exposure times were still being reckoned in seconds. A well-struck golf ball would have been almost out of sight in this time, travelling far too quickly to register a measurable image with the conventional equipment of the day. The problem would be solved by two individuals who were anything but conventional. They were almost exact contemporaries of Tait and their insights unlocked the secrets of animal and human locomotion by capturing perfect images of complex movement too fleeting to be resolved with the human eye.

Etienne-Jules Marey and Eadweard Muybridge shared exactly the same lifespan (1830–1904), very nearly the same as Tait's (1831–1901). There is no evidence to show that the three ever met, however, or that Tait was aware of their field of scientific interest. Marey and Muybridge certainly met, in Paris in 1861, at Marey's invitation. There they compared ideas on their differing approaches to the challenging subject of recording and analysing movement in all its contexts.

Tait would probably have rubbed along better with the Frenchman Marey. Compared with Muybridge he was more conventional, although no less gifted or inventive. He, like Tait, was an academic and had studied medicine at the University of Paris. He was also very skilled mechanically and invented devices for recording the human pulse and the wing beats of birds and insects.

Mechanical devices, however sensitive, are always invasive to some degree and may interfere with and modify the behaviour of the subject under scientific study. It seems that it was the meeting with Muybridge in 1861 that set Marey thinking about photography as the perfect way to capture movement without interfering in any way with the subject's behaviour. There was just one problem. Lightweight celluloid film would not appear until the 1880s and until then it was not possible to spool film rapidly through the camera. Marey solved this by using a circular photographic plate rotated at speed behind the camera lens, so successive still images of the moving subject could be captured. His original device was referred to as the 'fusil-photo', the 'rifle camera', an object it resembled closely, except that the barrel was a telephoto lens used to focus images on the rotating film plate. He must have appeared a strange sight as he mooched about the French countryside, but using the device he was able to reveal many of the subtleties of flight by freezing the rapid wing movements of birds. He also developed a very innovative method for recording human movement. His subjects wore black body-suits, with points such as ankles, knees and elbows identified by highly reflective buttons. The limb segments were picked out by joining these points with thin reflective strips. By filming against a very dark background only the buttons and reflective strips appeared in the image, producing a perfect record of the transient effects of human gait. These were the first examples of what are nowadays called kinetograms. At first sight they seem little more than animated matchstick men, but when the masses of the various limb segments are assigned, the subject's motion can be studied with great precision. Building a mathematical model derived from kinetograms enables 'what if' questions to be explored. What if this player inclines his body a little more at the instant of striking the ball? Will the ball's release speed be greater? And what if the goalkeeper takes a sideways step before diving to save a penalty; will that really improve his diving reach? Marey's principles can still be traced in highly sophisticated motion analysis systems in use today, although his reflective buttons have been replaced by infra-red transponders. The techniques are widely used to produce realistic animations in blockbuster films shot in cartoon format.

Muybridge was a much more eccentric individual. Born Eadweard James Muggeridge in Kingston-upon-Thames, he went to America in his twenties, returning to England briefly to study photography. In 1872 he formed a friendship with Leland Stanford, railway magnate and a governor of California. Muybridge, by then an established and skilled photographer, was persuaded to use his expertise to settle an ambitious bet made by Stanford with his business associates James R. Keene and Frederick MacCrellish. Some accounts put the figure as high as $25,000. Stanford, who made a fortune in railroad construction, could easily have afforded the loss but there is no record of any money changing hands. The bet concerned a horse's movements and the possibility (believed by Stanford) that during the gallop there was an instant when all four hooves were off the ground. The motion is too quick for the human eye and it took nearly six years to find conclusive proof and win the bet. In contrast to Marey's approach, Muybridge used multiple cameras, triggered in sequence as the horse galloped through trip wires.

The research was interrupted in 1874 when Muybridge was tried for murder. Always something of a volatile personality, he shot his wife's lover, suspecting that he was the father of their new-born son. The verdict was justifiable homicide but his acquittal may have owed something to Stanford's influence. Inevitably, perhaps, the pair later fell out when Stanford tried to claim credit for the work, painting Muybridge as a simple jour- neyman photographer. Muybridge was vindicated when he went on to produce many thousands of images and published his find- ings in several works including *Animal Locomotion* in 1887 and *The Human Figure in Motion* in 1901. Both he and Marey devel- oped devices that were the forerunners of moving film projectors and so were influential in the early development of film as an entertainment medium.

While Tait's ideas languished, the same could not be said of the contributions of Marey and Muybridge, but neither could have foreseen the pace at which the science of motion analysis would develop. Celluloid film was rapidly introduced and very fast emulsions meant that exposure times could be even shorter, rated in hundredths, even thousandths, rather than tenths of sec- onds. In the sports field coaches were quick to see the potential of the medium. Critical movements could be replayed and even shown in slow motion. But it was the possibility of quantitative analysis from film images that excited sports scientists. You can replay a film of a faulty action many times and often develop a remedy for the athlete; but what if the fault is subtle, accumu- lating from a sequence of many incorrect actions apparently insignificant in themselves, or if the coach and athlete wish to develop new techniques whose possible outcomes are uncertain, even dangerous? The only way to explore these questions is by developing an understanding not just of the motion but the underlying forces that are causing it. The science of biomechanics addresses these issues and it is a discipline that draws extensively on motion analysis as a tool in its application.

To describe any form of motion, the starting point is usually a precise knowledge of the forces that are acting. The fundamental problem was solved by Newton in the seventeenth century and expressed in the famous laws that bear his name. Simply stated, forces cause accelerations. The magnitude of the acceleration is obtained by dividing the known force by the mass of the object being pushed along. Knowing the acceleration, it is an easy step to find the object's speed at any instant and how far it will have moved in a given time. In football this would correspond to knowing just how much force is expended in the few thousandths of a second the foot is in contact with the ball. If it is kicked from rest it sails away with some initial speed and how far it goes depends on gravitational and aerodynamic forces. Simple in principle, but there's just one snag. Other than in highly artificial cases such as an object moving freely under gravity in the absence of air resistance, we rarely know the detailed form of the forces or how they change with time. And yet these are the very entities that the biomechanist is struggling to understand in the first place. This seems like a classic vicious circle.

To resolve this in practice, the trick is to work backwards, from effect to cause, from the observed motion to the forces responsible for it. We begin with very precise positional data obtained from a sequence of images recorded on film, or from video cameras. Accurate positional coordinates can be read directly from these, provided that the experimental space has been carefully calibrated. Knowing how fast the images were captured (the frame rate in filming) we then have a series of positions with the corresponding times it takes to reach them. These are easily turned into velocities (distance travelled per unit time) and into accelerations (velocity change per unit time). Newton's law is invoked once more but this time the accelerations are multiplied by the known mass of the object to produce the instantaneous forces. The process, a very powerful technique in biomechanics, is called 'inverse dynamics' simply because Newton's laws are applied in reverse. In the 1960s and 70s, Stanley Plagenhoef, a pioneer of human movement analysis, examined cine film images, frame by frame, and carefully digitised the positions of the limbs. The results were a series of accurately measured kinetograms (Fig. 4.1), very like Marey's, that could be used to determine the limb velocities and accelerations with great precision. These provided great insights into the mechanics of the skill of kicking, for example.

Photographic film as a research medium has largely been superseded by digital video imaging. There is simply no comparison between film and digital media where economics, ease of processing and sophistication of software analysis packages are the determining factors. It is remarkable just what measurement accuracy can be achieved in experimental studies of such activities as throws or free kicks, where the movement field extends over 20 metres or more.

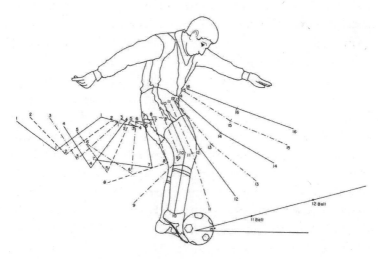

Fig. 4.1: Kinetogram digitised from cine film (after Plagenhoef)

There are also complementary systems for use where the field of view is more limited, say, a few metres rather than tens of metres. These do not produce visible images but are capable of very high accuracy, often measuring positions to fractions of a millimetre. The principle is very like Marey's body-suit kinetograms; subjects wear lightweight sensors attached to key parts of their anatomy. A recording station emits infra-red pulses at very high frequency and the sensors respond with their instantaneous positional coordinates. A huge benefit of systems of this kind is that no digitising of sequential images is necessary to obtain positional coordinates. All this is taken care of in the software analysis package linked to the data capture system. Rather like digital imaging, however, the initial results come in the form of positions, velocities and accelerations, so it is still necessary to use some form of inverse dynamics to get at the all-important forces.

Systems like these, whether based on digital imaging or using infra-red transponders, have contributed enormously to the understanding of human movement in the widest sense in sport and greatly aided the development of the science of biomechanics. It took many decades before systems of today's complexity evolved, but from the 1950s onwards there were signs that other disciplines in the sports field had shaken off their torpor when a trickle of serious scientific papers began to emerge.

Perhaps appropriately, the first of these returned to the theme of ball flight that had so fascinated Tait, but this time covering both baseball and golf. Football had to wait until the early 1960s for serious quantitative study, but two papers from that era stand out. One deals with players' perceptions of their goal-scoring abilities and is seldom cited in the scientific literature, but it contains some intriguing insights. The other, a statistical study of passing movements and goal-scoring, is regularly referenced and it influenced thinking about football profoundly, the English game especially. Let us look at each in turn.

In 1962 two psychologists, John Cohen and E. J. Dearnaley

from the University of Manchester, published a paper entitled 'Skill and judgement of footballers in attempting to score goals'. They defined their paper as a study in 'psychological probability' but it was no excursion into woolly thinking or jargonising. These authors posed a very concrete research question: how good are footballers at predicting the positions at which they will convert a stated proportion of their shots into goals? To take some extremes we might guess that shots fail 100 per cent of the time from beyond 35 metres (38 yards), but all should succeed a few metres from goal. How does the probability change between these extremes and, equally important, how good are strikers at making this assessment in a match situation?

This paper interested me greatly. In the late 1960s I was exploring an important 'set play' between the striker and the goalkeeper, the so-called goalkeeper/attacker 'one-on-one', where the defence has been breached and a lone attacker races towards goal with only the goalkeeper left to beat. Exactly where and when the shot came would provide valuable data to validate my model and these researchers seemed to have constructed the scenario perfectly. To carry out their study Cohen and Dearnaley enlisted two elite teams, Manchester United and West Bromwich Albion, and two amateur sides from Manchester University and a local Manchester school. Thirty-three players in all were involved, 20 from the elite clubs and 13 from the amateur teams. Today's practitioners in sports science might smile at these proportions, especially at the greater number of elite professionals who were willing to assist the researchers. Nowadays it is sometimes difficult to recruit even gifted amateurs as research subjects.

The study ran as follows. With observers in attendance, the players were asked to advance from their own halves towards the opponents' goal straight down the centre. The goalkeeper stood on the goal line. They were asked to stop at the position where they felt they could score once if they made a hundred attempts. The position was marked, then the striker moved on to where he felt his chances were 1 in 5, then 2 in 5, up to the point where he was confident of scoring every time. The players were then returned to these positions and the actual success rates measured for five shots attempted from each location.

Fig. 4.2 shows the outcomes and compares the players' assessments of their forecast scoring ability with their actual achievements. As might be expected the forecasts are a little optimistic but in general the correlation is quite good. The chance of scoring rises from effectively zero at roughly 30 metres from goal to dead certainty at 6 metres. Just on the edge of the penalty area attackers converted 40 per cent of shots, and interestingly, the chance of scoring from the penalty distance, 11 metres, is 70 per cent, very much in line with the conversion rates for penalty kicks studied in detail nearly four decades after this work.

Another important series of measurements was made when the goalkeeper was allowed to vary his tactics by leaving his line

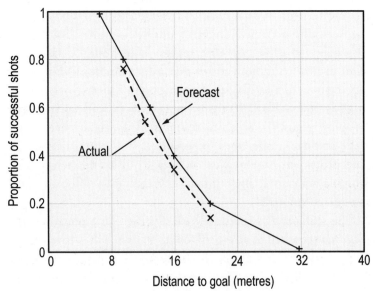

Fig. 4.2: Footballer's predicted and actual scoring rates
(after Cohen and Dearnaley)

to counter the threat. Three distinct patterns emerged: the striker shot at some distance from the goalkeeper, close to the goalkeeper, or by dribbling around the goalkeeper and shooting at an empty net. More than half of the goals scored came when the goalkeeper was slow in leaving his line. The least desirable option from the striker's point of view was where the goalkeeper got out quickly, approaching close enough to deter or block the shot. These results informed my thinking on the goalkeeper/attacker 'one-on-one' significantly. The goalkeeper's best strategy appeared to be to close the shooting opportunity right down and a way of defining this important position exactly in my model emerged from the geometry of the players' positions in relation to the goalposts. For the goalkeeper, movement off the line was better than waiting for the inevitable shot, even though this might involve the forward attempting to dribble round the goalkeeper. And even in this case there would be a better chance of pulling off a diving save as the forward attempted to run past.

Cohen and Dearnaley had some limited success in verifying their findings by analysing film of actual matches. One of these was the famous 1960 European Cup final between Real Madrid and Eintracht Frankfurt. The problem was that, although there were plenty of goals (Real Madrid won 7–3, Puskas scoring four, di Stéfano three), most of the time Real Madrid were banging them in from inside the penalty area, so the basic assumption of a lone attacker bearing down on goal with an isolated keeper scarcely applied. Film, we have seen, is not the best medium for rapidly extracting ad hoc information and there were almost no opportunities in the 1960s for recording televised matches so that specific incidents could be analysed in detail later. Their study was nevertheless revealing and would bear repeating given the abundance of today's information sources.

The second key investigation in these early scientific studies of football was that in 1968 by Charles Reep and Bernard Benjamin, who looked at passing and shooting in their paper 'Skill and chance in association football'. The data collected for this work had been assembled over many years by Reep, a former RAF wing commander, who had invented a shorthand method for recording every on-the-ball sequence during the course of a match. Reep was very much ahead of his time and his notation system and match analysis methods preceded similar efforts by almost two decades. His work in the early 1950s and his success in managing various RAF teams soon came to the attention of the professional game. Brentford, then a Second Division side facing relegation, were rescued by Reep's interventions and he went on to work with success as a consultant, first with Wolverhampton Wanderers in the 1950s and then with Watford in the 1970s.

In his study with Benjamin, a total of 578 games between 1953 and 1967, involving a spread of top English League matches and two World Cups, were recorded in detail. A subject of intense interest then, as today, was possession, and a vital question concerned how long a passing sequence could be sustained before it broke down. The results are shown in Fig. 4.3. Long sequences do not occur often and the chances of putting together a really long string of passes are very small in practice. Of course we all remember fabulous build-ups leading to spectacular goals, but many thousands of routine, boring exchanges of possession have been erased from that highly selective and fallible mechanism we call memory.

It is worth looking at the figures. Movements involving as few as four passes occurred only 5 per cent of the time in their study. Six passes or more form a very small proportion, around 1 per cent of the total. The reason for this is clear. Long chains of passes require repeated accuracy, very difficult to sustain as defenders move in to close down space and man-mark the targets as the sequence stretches out.

Two other key statistics came out of this work. Reep and Benjamin showed that around 80 per cent of all goals scored resulted from three passes or fewer and that the ratio of goals to shooting attempts came out at nearly 1 in 10. The results have

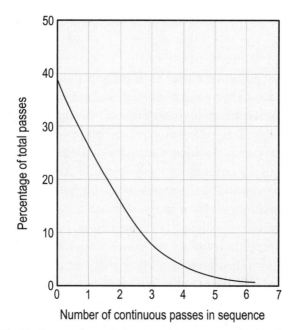

Fig. 4.3: Chance of completing a passing sequence of a given length (after Reep and Benjamin)

been broadly confirmed whenever passing and shooting have been investigated, leading to the suspicion that these numbers may be pointing to something more fundamental in the game. Distance from goal is an important factor, as Cohen and Dearnaley showed, and perhaps it is also related to the fact that very often there is only a limited area of the goal to shoot at. Some may feel that arguments like these are pushing the statistical nature of the game too far. Whatever the reasons, no one has come close to an explanation.

There is no doubt that Reep and Benjamin's findings had a major impact on the game, especially in England, producing intense debate and resulting in some clubs playing what came to be called the 'direct' or 'long ball' game. Getting the ball into the opponents' penalty area as quickly as possible was the objective; it was often sarcastically said that the tactic made up for lack of expertise in midfield – the ball seldom lingered there – and perhaps significantly it never caught on at international level. Wolves' and Watford's success was due in some measure to Reep's method, but he was traduced by the English press, who found hard to swallow the concept that statistical chance played a material part in the beautiful game. His case was not helped by the fact that some of the sides who espoused his principles (but with whom he was never directly associated) played the long ball game practically to the exclusion of anything else. Wimbledon was one such. At one period in the top flight in English football, their home games attracted fewer supporters than many teams playing several leagues below them. Their method was described as the 'route one' approach and its Wimbledon exponents, because of the energy and frequency with which they launched themselves and the ball into the penalty area, were nicknamed 'the Crazy Gang' after a troupe of six comedians who mixed circus acrobatics with slapstick and had played at the London Palladium in the 1930s.

Cohen and Dearnaley's and Reep and Benjamin's studies shed considerable light on the game in the 1960s but neither would have given a coach much insight into the physiological demands of the various team positions. Starting with a card of 11 players, how should they most suitably be fitted into the classic roles demanded by defence (including the goalkeeper), midfield and attack? Skill, strength and speed would be obvious factors, but what about the stamina required for each position? Do defenders work harder than attackers and do midfielders, as we would probably suspect, work hardest of all? There were some conflicting views but not until a seminal paper on this topic appeared in 1976 could the questions be answered confidently. This was published by two researchers, Thomas Reilly and Vaughan Thomas from Liverpool Polytechnic (now Liverpool John Moores University), and entitled 'A motion analysis of work-rate in different positional roles in professional football match-play'.

Prior to this there had been numerous attempts to quantify

the distances covered by players during the course of a game. Estimates varied widely, ranging from 17 km to only 4.8 km. Intuitively, such extremes appear unlikely. To a very good approximation the distance covered during a match is a measure of the players' energy expenditure. Differences like these would imply enormous variation in metabolic loading and corresponding fitness, and while we have all seen frenetic matches, it would be a very one-sided contest if one team's players covered, on average, more than three times the distance of the opposition.

To carry out their work Reilly and Thomas were supported by one of the top English First Division clubs (equivalent to the Premiership in today's organisation). All roles were covered in the assessment: full backs, centre backs, midfielders, strikers and goalkeepers. The chosen team played 4-3-3 at that time. Defining the playing style is important as this can influence the work-rate requirement of individual positions appreciably. This factor has not yet been studied in depth for today's commonly used playing formations and is often overlooked when work-rate issues are under discussion.

Reilly and Thomas divided movement patterns into discrete categories: jogging, cruising, sprinting, walking and backing. Most of these are familiar concepts. Cruising was defined as 'running with manifest purpose and effort'. More localised activities such as jumping for headers and saves, or standing still, whether resting or injured, were also logged. To estimate distances covered at home games the familiar field markings were used but, in addition, lines were painted on the walls at the sides of the pitch, effectively forming grid markers. For away matches convenient points on advertising hoardings were used and were again related to the pitch markings. A complete season was studied, embracing 51 competitive games in total with one specific player being observed in each match. Data was hand-logged, supplemented by voice using a portable tape recorder. A key requirement was that assessments based on grid markings on the pitch could be used to give an accurate measure of the distance actually covered. To achieve this, subjects were filmed at each of the matches studied, and stride frequencies obtained for each of the characteristic movements such as jogging, sprinting, etc. In all forms of running, subjects generally use the same stride frequency but change the stride length to go faster. It was simply then a question of accurately measuring each subject's mean stride length during training when jogging, sprinting or cruising. Then, by counting the number of steps in the filmed sequences, distance covered in the various running modes could accurately be determined. The error in measuring distance in this way was estimated as only 1 per cent, acceptable precision for an evaluation of this kind given that subjects typically cover many kilometres in a game.

The results of the study were revealing. In each game a player executes around 1,000 individual playing sequences involving switches between the different movement profiles (resting, jogging, sprinting, etc.) as well as specific activities such as heading and tackling. These switches in activity occur, on average, every 5 to 6 seconds and rest periods last as little as 3 seconds every 2 minutes or so. Sprinting distances averaged out at 15 metres and occurred at intervals of 90 seconds.

Football is often called a possession game but in Reilly and Thomas's study it was revealed that the 10 outfield players are actually in contact with the ball for only 2 per cent of the total distance they cover in a match. The game is really played off the ball, and anyone who fixes attention on the player in possession is missing a huge proportion of the game. This applies not just to spectators but players also. 'Ball watching' is a severe criticism of a defender who fails to pick up a key attacking movement that develops off the ball.

The distances covered by players in each position are shown in Fig. 4.4. Of the outfield players, midfielders easily carry the burden of the team's work-rate, in this study getting through an average of 9.8 km per match. Centre backs by comparison average 7.8 km, although more of this distance is covered by backing or sideways movements compared with other positions. Strikers

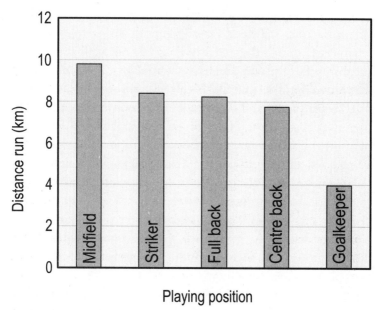

Fig. 4.4: Distance covered in various playing positions (after Reilly and Thomas)

and full backs are fairly comparable in terms of total distance covered at 8.4 km and 8.2 km respectively, but there was a difference in the observed movement patterns for these playing roles. The greatest variability in total distance covered over the season was observed for full backs (eight in all were involved in the study) indicating that work-rate is very much a function of the playing tactics adopted. If tactics require the full backs to play defensively, the movement profile will be much more like that of the centre back. In going forward on overlapping runs, however, the full backs' profile will be much more like a midfielder's and a greater distance would be covered compared with a defensive role. There was also a marked difference when first- and second-half comparisons were made. Taking all the movement components (jogging, cruising and sprinting), 73 per cent of all outfield players showed a second-half decline due to fatigue, significantly shorter distances being achieved.

The goalkeeper deserves a separate profile given the uniqueness of the role. Reilly and Thomas showed that this player covers nearly 4 km during the course of the game, which is at first sight surprising for a player effectively confined to the penalty area. The activity profile contrasts sharply with that of outfield players. The keeper has far and away the most possession, spending just over 10 per cent of the 4 km with the ball, and covers 25 per cent of his total distance moving backwards. This is about double the average for all outfield players. Taking all activities and movements into account the goalkeeper has more direct involvement in the play than any outfield player.

Reilly and Thomas's study is often taken as the standard for work-rate assessment in football. No subsequent research has negated any of their findings for the relative distances covered in each playing position, although today's players can expect to run nearly 30 per cent further on average. This and subsequent research has had enormous implications over the years for quantifying the physiological demands of the game, as we shall see in a moment. So too for match analysis techniques, pioneered by Mike Hughes and his co-workers of the University of Wales Institute, Cardiff. These early studies have increased in sophistication and notational analysis – as the discipline is now called – has grown into a formidable research tool for understanding games in general and football in particular.

There are many reasons for wanting to reduce a game such as football to some form of codified format, but two in particular stand out. The first is the need to break the game down into identifiable elements, much in the manner of the early studies, to improve fundamental understanding. The second is so that accurate reference points identifying good and bad performance can be established, to guide coaches in improving individual or team effectiveness. Memory is a very unreliable device either way. As Reilly and Thomas showed, any given player completes nearly 1,000 discrete activities during the course of a game. Many are repeated, perhaps in extended cycles, but this is irrelevant.

Memory recall tends to be subjective and attempting to identify key performance indicators for a particular player using memory alone is prone to error. A trivial example illustrates the point. Casual observation of a game may lead to the conclusion that one striker is better than another because he scored more goals. A deeper analysis might reveal that the 'inferior' player, in fact, converted more of his chances without adequate support from midfield. A formal notation system should be superior to ad hoc recall and if properly constructed will ensure performance indicators are normative, so that valid comparisons can be made. In other words, Striker X didn't just score 2 goals, but converted 10 per cent of his chances. Similarly, Winger Y found the near post with 60 per cent of his in-swinging corners.

Valuable though the early notation systems were, they suffered from disadvantages that restricted widespread application. Learning a manual notation system is not a trivial skill and it takes time to reach the kind of proficiency required to follow a match in real time. There is also the added burden of interpreting the records and reducing them to a format where meaningful analysis can be carried out. Both processes were transformed by using computers for these purposes but not before better ways of entering data were devised. The standard keyboard is not very user-friendly in this respect as few people have adequate typing skills and manual notation would generally be more efficient. The real gains came when the computer interface was improved, first by configuring the keyboard so that individual keys mimicked the layout of a pitch (keyboard mapping), and then by using overlay keyboards as the direct means of data entry. These devices are touch-sensitive flat boards, usually A3 or A4 in format, which replace the conventional keyboard. Data can be entered simply by touching a point on the surface, programmed to represent a specific location or action. This gives much higher resolution than a system relying on keyboard mapping, for example. The trick is to define an overlay representing the physical layout of the pitch, with areas of the board dedicated to specific actions on the part of the players. Hughes, Robertson and Nicholson (1988) used an overlay keyboard covering the standard pitch markings with touch-sensitive areas to represent standard actions such as passes, corners and free kicks. In this way they analysed in great detail patterns of play in the 1986 World Cup. A similar approach was adopted by Partridge and Franks to study crosses in the same competition from various parts of the pitch into specific zones in and around the penalty area. Even this form of data entry has been superseded and it is now possible to define pitch overlays directly on-screen using graphical user interfaces, so that data can be entered using mouse clicks or even voice-actuated commands.

There have been many applications of notational analysis in football but three specific examples illustrate the power of the technique and the insights it can provide, whether team or individual performances are concerned.

In the 1990 World Cup competition in Italy, West Germany beat Argentina 1–0 in the final and England and Italy played for third and fourth places. Italy won 2–1, so the final ranking was West Germany, Argentina, Italy, England. In analysing this tournament, Luhtanen (1993) was interested in how teams played in the attacking third, specifically how often a team that retained possession in this key zone followed on to a scoring attempt and how successful these were. To do this he used a pitch overlay and devised a notation system for matches observed live, via live television and from recordings. His detailed results covered the top four teams mentioned above, and his analysis confirmed that West Germany's winning performance was no fluke. The team was easily the strongest, assessed in terms of retained possession and the number of chances converted. They kept the ball in 69 per cent of all attacks. Some 37 per cent of this possession led to scoring chances and in turn, 10 per cent of these produced goals. By comparison, England's figures were 67 per cent, 26 per cent and 12 per cent respectively. In other words, they retained almost as much possession in the

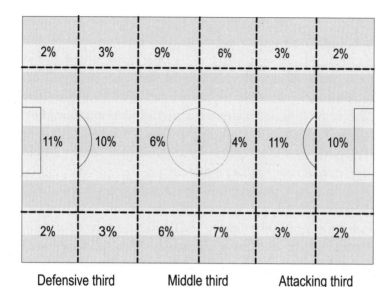

| | | |
| Defensive third | Middle third | Attacking third |

Fig. 4.5: Injury frequencies as a function of pitch location
(after Rahnama, Reilly and Lees)

final third and converted slightly more of their chances, but created fewer chances overall. Interestingly also, for the whole tournament the ratio of goals to shots at goal was 1 in 9.3, very close to Reep's magic ratio.

The second example addresses the important question of injury potential. What sort of playing actions are most injury-prone, when are they most likely to occur during a game and where are the most dangerous locations on the pitch in this respect? Three researchers from Liverpool John Moores University, Rahnama, Reilly and Lees, set out to answer these questions by looking at 10 games in the English Premiership between 1999 and 2000. They developed a notation system based on a pitch divided into 18 zones (Fig. 4.5). This is similar to the conventional 9 zone division of Fig. 2.6 (shown in Chapter 2), with the attacking, middle and defensive thirds further divided in half. Their notational scheme embraced the 16 common actions of the game, including dribbling, heading, tackling, shooting and throwing. In the 10 games they studied, 17,877 discrete actions based on the 16 classifications were recorded, 43 per cent of which (7,667) were judged to have injury potential of some kind (mild, moderate or high). This implies an overall rate of 53 injuries per 1,000 hours played for the various types, although serious injuries occur at a much lower rate, perhaps about a tenth of this figure. Fans all around the world will know that certain 'grudge matches' attract a much greater proportion of this kind of injury.

The activities producing the greatest likelihood of injury in what could be called 'normal' play occur not surprisingly in launching or receiving tackles, and the risk is greatest during the first and last 15 minutes of the match. Most spectators would agree that this is intuitively right: the opening phases of any game are usually played at high tempo, sometimes at a frantic pace, whereas by the closing stage of the game, fatigue will have taken its toll. Both states are likely to blunt the precision required in timing a tackle perfectly and injury frequently follows as a consequence.

The final question addressed by the research concerned how injury potential varied in different locations on the pitch. From the 7,667 incidents recorded it is possible to plot the observed frequencies in the zones in which they occurred (cf. Fig. 4.5). These are significantly higher in the central region of the attacking and defending thirds, precisely the locations where defenders must neutralise the attacking threat if goals are to be prevented. Obviously, penalty considerations aside, defenders are not likely to hold back, given what is at stake, and an enhanced rate of injury-related tackling can be expected.

By contrast with the previous two examples, Gerisch and Reichelt's research in 1993 looked at a much more specific aspect of the game. They studied outfield-player 'one-on-one' encounters where two players contested possession of the ball, in the important European Cup semi-final in April 1991 between Bayern Munich and Red Star Belgrade. In their notation scheme the target actions were defined as headers, fouls, possessions won or lost, and intention reached or failed. By this latter category was meant such things as making or blocking shots and centres. These kinds of encounters are much more taxing in energy terms than conventional play, involving more frequent sprints and jumps. In addition to logging the events in relation to the usual pitch zones (defensive, midfield and attacking thirds plus the centre, left and right laterals), Gerisch and Reichelt super-imposed a time code on the data so that one-on-ones could be tracked throughout the progress of the match. There were 250 such encounters, exactly 125 each, suggesting superficially that the game was balanced, but the important consideration con-cerned which team won the encounter and how the workload was spread among the individual players. Examination of the progression of these throughout the match shows that Red Star used their possession more profitably than Bayern. After initial pressure leading to an early goal, Bayern's dominance evapor-ated. Red Star pressed home their advantage and equalised just before half-time.

Bender, the Bayern midfielder who was generally acknow-ledged to be out of position when Red Star equalised, had been exposed to 18 gruelling one-on-ones in 25 minutes and through-out the match had won only 29 per cent of these encounters. He simply could not recover his position when Red Star broke through for the equaliser. By contrast, Prosinecki for Red Star gave an acknowledged master performance in midfield and turned the game for his side. His one-on-one performance was in stark contrast to Bender's. He won 59 per cent of his encounters and was still running at the final whistle. Although Bayern rallied and began to perform better in the one-on-ones towards the end of the game, they could not turn their final period of dominance into a goal, and were caught on the break by Red Star who ran out 2–1 winners. They became European Champions, eventually beating Olympique de Marseille in a penalty shoot-out in the 1991 final.

Bender's unfortunate semi-final experience with Red Star brings home forcibly the fact that football is a physically demanding, often draining experience at the highest level. This was clear from Reilly and Williams' work-rate assessments, endorsed in all the subsequent studies that looked at the physiological demands of the game. To run approaching 10 km in 90 minutes and to intersperse this activity with punishing sprints, twists and jumps taxes the body's metabolism severely. What exactly is the motor driving this effort, and, equally important, what is the fuel sustaining this prodigious effort?

The answer to the first question is easy. There is only one agency in human physiology that drives physical activity – the muscle groups responsible for movement. Since muscle fibres can only *contract*, they have to be disposed over the skeleton in such a way that sometimes they open a limb segment and sometimes close it, exactly the cycle of muscle movements involved in running or jumping, for example. The extent of muscle contraction, in other words the strength of the force controlling the movement, depends on the rate of nerve impulses sent to the muscle; the greater the rate the bigger the contraction and the greater the force that can be applied. With repeated hard exertion muscle groups tend to shorten and this is why players stretch during pre-match warm ups and after the matches to avoid the possibility of muscle damage.

The biological system that produces movement is chemical in origin. A substance stored in the muscle groups called adenosine triphosphate, ATP for short, is broken down into adenosine diphosphate, ADP, which triggers muscular contraction. It is a case of one form of energy, chemical, being transformed into another, mechanical, although as the conversion can never be 100 per cent efficient a small amount of energy is lost in the form of heat. The chemical reaction is very fast, but not much ATP is distributed throughout the musculature. This means that it must be constantly replenished to sustain physical exercise. There are just two ways to do this. The body can either produce ATP from aerobic sources, i.e. oxygen breathed in as part of sustained exercise, or for the more intensive burst of energy from chemical storage within the muscle groups themselves, so-called anaerobic sources.

Aerobic replenishment of ATP is the most important source of energy consumption in football as perhaps 90 per cent of the energy required throughout the game is provided this way. The analogy with a conventional engine, burning fuel in combination with oxygen, is almost exact. Fats, carbohydrates and to a very small extent protein are combined with oxygen breathed from the air and are transported in the bloodstream to the muscle cells. How efficient this process is depends on an individual's cardio-vascular system. It is often quoted as the $\dot{V}O_2$ index and defines the volume of oxygen consumed per unit time and per unit of body mass. The maximum capacity for oxygen utilisation, $\dot{V}O_{2max}$, is a measure of ultimate fitness in aerobic exercise and figures of 4.5 litres per minute would not be unusual for the top performers. This rate cannot not be sustained for an entire match, but estimates have shown that outfield players perform at a level approaching 75 per cent of $\dot{V}O_{2max}$ throughout, the equivalent figure for the less demanding role of goalkeeper being about 50 per cent.

Techniques for measuring oxygen uptake during exercise tend to be invasive, involving the wearing of respirators, and so determining metabolic stress under actual match conditions using such equipment is not really feasible. Fortunately there is another route. Measurements can be made under laboratory conditions, in treadmill running for example, and correlated with heart rate. Then by fitting players with lightweight heart rate monitors which can transmit the information by radio, $\dot{V}O_2$ determinations during the real games can be estimated with fair precision. In 1983 Van Gool, Van Gerven and Boutmans measured heart rates in beats per minute for outfield players and reported average values of 155 (centre backs), 155 (full backs), 170 (midfielders) and 171 (forwards). These figures are very much in line with Reilly and Thomas's work-rate estimates, based on the total distance covered in these specific positions.

The really intensive activities in a competitive match last only about 7 minutes in total for each player and are split into very short duration bursts. For example, some 20 sprints, each around 2 seconds' duration, will occur in this period in addition to many sudden accelerations, stops, feints and jumps. Even an apparently innocuous activity like dribbling taxes fitness significantly. This was demonstrated by Reilly and Ball (1984), who were able to simulate dribbling during a treadmill exercise by arranging for the ball to be returned to the exercising athlete by a rebound board mounted at the front of the treadmill. These researchers showed that dribbling while running at 4 metres per second increased energy consumption by 7 per cent compared with simply running at the same speed. This is a significant margin taken over the duration of a hard game.

For these infrequent, intensive actions the rate of energy supply by oxygen uptake is insufficient and the muscle groups draw on internal sources to supply the deficit. This is known as anaerobic loading and there are two limited reservoirs when the aerobic limit is reached. In the first, the breakdown of the compound creatine phosphate in the muscle fibres themselves is the source. The second relies on the decomposition of glycogen (glucose or sugar molecules), a substance derived from carbohydrates in the diet and again stored in muscle tissue. A consequence of this latter reaction is the production of lactic acid, and sampling for lactates in the blood can also give a good indication of anaerobic stress during a game.

Given these factors, what is the energy cost per match of playing football at the top level? As already noted, elite players have measured $\dot{V}O_{2max}$ capacities approaching 4.5 litres per minute, so for an average loading of 75 per cent of this throughout the game the total energy consumption can be estimated at about 1,700 kilo-calories (kcal). This energy, expended in 90 minutes, is about 67 per cent of the recommended *daily* dietary requirement for the average healthy male. Sweating alone produces a weight loss of between 2 and 2.5 kg in a hard contest. These findings point to important dietary considerations.

For players training regularly and playing a competitive game once per week the average energy intake depends on body mass, but will be between 3,000 and 3,500 kcal per day. Female players at the top level require around 500–600 fewer kcal than this. The most important component of a balanced diet involving protein, fats and carbohydrates is the latter, as these substances are essential for replenishment of glycogen stores in the body. Pasta, rice, bread and potatoes are the most important sources. However, pre-match meals should not be 'blow-outs' for many reasons. Excessive carbohydrate intake is unnecessary at this stage and would add little to the already replenished stores of glycogen. So a snack beforehand is all that is necessary. After the game the body's store of glycogen content is depleted, but the capacity for replenishment is at a maximum for the first few hours, declining speedily thereafter. Carbohydrate drinks taken quickly can greatly assist the renewal process. This can be followed by a post-match snack, then a meal. In this way glycogen stores can be renewed within 24 hours, important if competitive games are to be played at short intervals.

Fluid intake is also essential for hard training and to compensate for fluid loss during matches. There are many proprietary drinks but fluid containing simply sugar, in a concentration of around 6 per cent, plus a small amount of sodium salt is sufficient. This simple mixture is preferable to water alone. The daily fluid intake should be around 2–3 litres taken continuously and not simply in response to promptings from thirst, which is not a good indicator of fluid replenishment needs.

In addition to carbohydrate replenishment, sports dieticians also look at protein, vitamin and mineral requirements. Although protein intake does not need to be high (up to around 100 gm per day is acceptable), problems can occur during periods of sustained, intense exercise. At such times some of the energy requirement is satisfied by a depletion of the body's store of amino acids, the main constituents of protein. The problems become acute only when this energy deficit persists over sustained periods. The implications are more serious for women and junior players, and unless the problem is recognised and remedied, players can become more prone to injury and illness.

On the topic of vitamin and mineral requirements there has been much intense debate and the modern consensus is that a balanced diet contains almost everything necessary for high-intensity competition. The one exception is iron, as small quantities are excreted in sweat and urine. The uptake of iron in even a balanced diet is usually fairly low, but this is easily remedied if iron deficiency occurs. Uptake improves when iron is combined with vitamin C; or iron can be taken in controlled amounts in tablet form.

Football has come a long way from the basic game of the 1860s with its earnest amateur players and just 14 simple rules. Today the game is played more skilfully and at a much higher tempo, changes that have been brought about largely because of the scientific insights introduced from the middle of the last century. There is scarcely an aspect of football that has not been touched in this way and there is more to come. One urgent question concerns the issue of player 'burn-out' as international matches and European games pile on top of gruelling domestic commitments. The wealthiest clubs can simply double up their squads, but others may look to the sports scientists for more affordable solutions. We are likely to see carefully structured training regimes tailored to the intensity of weekly competition but planned around the cycle of a full season's commitments. Recovery periods for key players will feature strongly in such programmes.

Footballers of the future will look back on today's methods with the same amusement we reserve for training sessions of half a century ago: endless lapping of the pitch in search of that elusive quantity, stamina, and not a ball in sight until Saturday's game.

CHAPTER 5

MOTIVATION OR MIND GAMES – THE PSYCHOLOGICAL DIMENSION

On 25 May 2005 AC Milan and Liverpool played what has come to be considered the most enthralling European Cup final in the history of the competition, perhaps the very best in modern times. It was not comparable as a spectacle with the foot-balling display served up in 1960 by Real Madrid when they beat Eintracht Frankfurt 7–3, and not (with due deference to their first-half performance) like the skills a previous AC Milan team displayed in sweeping aside FC Barcelona 4–0 in 1994. It was, though, the only occasion in a European Cup final when a team, certainly outplayed in the first half, had overcome a 3-goal deficit, and by dint of immense courage and almost super-human physical endurance forged a fresh start in winning through to a penalty shoot-out. What the world then saw was a perfect example of the winning mindset. Liverpool were mentally tougher and played all the psychological cards in their hand to perfection.

They needed just a little assistance. A recovering Milan had become ominously threatening in extra time. In the final minute Andriy Shevchenko rose and headed at almost point-blank range; Jerzy Dudek, goalkeeper for Liverpool, could only parry the ball and when Shevchenko followed up with a shot, looked beaten. But he made a marvellous reflex save which would have import-ant repercussions. In that split second Milan, and Shevchenko especially, received a devastating psychological blow in being denied a certain winning goal. Dudek and Liverpool by contrast were immensely lifted. The importance of this exchange would be revealed when Dudek and Shevchenko faced up in a make-or-break penalty kick in the shoot-out that came very shortly afterwards.

The job of the coach at this important point in a tied game is to select a group of players who can finish the job. He must also find a way to instil confidence, by preparing them mentally for the individual challenges to come. Rafael Benítez, Liverpool's coach, was aware of two daunting facts at that stage: Liverpool had missed 7 of their last 15 penalties, whereas just two years previously AC Milan had triumphed over Juventus in the European final, dominating the shoot-out. The Milan keeper, Nelson de Jesus Dida, had saved three penalties on that occasion and given his big-match temperament might be fancied to do the same again. Fortunately for Liverpool, Benítez is unexcitable, exuding calm under pressure. These are *not* the occasions for scarifying, dominating pep-talks when what players need is to be settled, so that they can become completely focused on the task they will shortly have to perform.

If Benítez was calmness personified the complete opposite was being played out just a few steps away where the television images captured goalkeeper Dudek being harangued by one of Liverpool's heroes, Jamie Carragher. With much arm waving and gesticulation, Carragher is exhorting Dudek to 'Remember Brucie'. This refers to the notorious incident when Bruce Grobbelaar, Liverpool keeper in the 1984 European Cup final in Rome, had performed his famous rubber-legged dance on the goal line, psyching the Roma penalty taker into a wasted shot. Dudek looks at Carragher, relaxed and amused but nevertheless taking it all in. He is at this stage 'in flow', perfectly attuned to the impending task, thanks to his miracle saves of a moment ago. These occasions occur when athletes feel absolutely in control, confident of handling anything the game can throw at them. At such times psychological arousal motivates rather than throttles performance. Fortunately, Carragher would not be added to the list of penalty takers for Liverpool although he would doubtless have stepped up if the team needed him. Unlike Dudek, he was both physically exhausted and dangerously 'pumped up', in no shape to despatch the kind of clinical delivery needed to guarantee success.

In recorded playbacks we can see that Dudek further demonstrates his composure and control as he meets the Milan keeper Dida at the goal chosen for the shoot-out. Milan's support is concentrated here. Dudek does not need to psych his opposite number in any way. He is saving that for the actual shoot-out and the players he will face then. So what the supporters see are simply two players sharing the camaraderie of the severest test any goalkeeper can face.

With Serginho of Milan lined up for the first penalty, Dudek makes an important move. He walks off his line to the penalty spot and attempts an exchange with Serginho. The referee will have none of it and waves Dudek back. What Dudek wants to do is remind Serginho of his physical presence: 'Look, it's me. I've just made a fantastic save from your best striker and in a second or so *your* reputation's on the line!' Dudek walks back into position and after turning to face Serginho begins an extraordinary performance, throwing himself wildly about, up and down the goal line. This is Grobbelaar in the extreme, but it is a very careful calculation. Dudek needs to keep his arousal just at the right pitch and vigorous movement is a good way of achieving this. He is also demonstrating to Serginho just how much of the goal he's got covered. If the striker was unsettled by the first move he is now rattled and his focus shifts dangerously. He should be thinking confidently about the fundamentals of his task: his run-up to the ball, a good contact and the shot hitting the net. Instead he is being forced to watch these stupid antics! He glances across at the referee, but there is no help from that quarter. What Dudek is doing is highly unorthodox but quite legal. So Serginho thinks, 'I'll put a stop to this – I'll blast it by him so hard he won't get a sniff.' And, predictably, he hammers the ball high over the bar.

When Dida faces Liverpool's first penalty it is a complete contrast. He waits in the middle of the goal, hands at his sides, virtually immobile until the final few strides of the striker's run-up. He makes absolutely no attempt to engage in 'verbals' with the penalty takers. In 2003 he played a big part in Milan's victory although one of his three saves was from a disgracefully illegal encroachment when he moved forward off his line before the ball was struck. Perhaps this is why he is so static now. In the event, Dietmar Hamman's cool shot gives him no chance and Milan are in trouble. This is not irrecoverable but they must convert the next penalty to stay in touch with Liverpool. Their players, waiting their turn in the centre circle, begin to feel the pressure, but must attempt to shut these disquieting images out and get back to focused thinking. Andrea Pirlo, next for Milan, does not inspire confidence with his anxious expression. Significantly also, Dudek is waiting for him ball in hand, and he marches out to the spot to present it to Pirlo. What can the referee do to prevent such an apparently courteous act? Dudek has now succeeded in physically closing on his opponent and in handing over the ball is effectively saying, 'This is mine, but I'm giving you permission to have a go. Let's see if you can do any better than your mate who's just missed.' Pirlo waits nervously until Dudek turns, then the familiar antics on the goal line start again. Unlike Serginho, Pirlo won't hang about but he too is clearly unsettled and any focus or confidence he'd mustered has now gone. Before he reaches the ball, Dudek leaves his line and that is the factor that decides it. Pirlo, conscious of the early move, chokes and hits a weak shot, easily saved by Dudek. This illegal penalty should really have been retaken, and had this happened it might have been the factor that finally shifted momentum back to Milan. But referee Mejuto Gonzalez gives the goal and his official, standing as an observer on the dead-ball line, has no objection. It is entirely possible that the officials have also been so distracted by Dudek's antics that the illegal encroachment on the shot has gone unnoticed.

Milan are now deeply in trouble. Although the deficit is reduced when John Arne Riise of Liverpool misses his shot, Shevchenko arrives for Milan's final penalty knowing that he *has* to score simply to make Liverpool take their last one. He too will receive the full treatment from Dudek, probably combined with disquieting memories of what had happened a few moments earlier when he missed an open goal. Since then Dudek has saved twice and his confidence is sky high.

The slow-motion video replay tells the story. Dudek goes through the 'hail fellow, well met' routine, but as he is about to hand the ball over takes a step back so Shevchenko is forced to reach for it. How much more emphatically could Dudek show that he is now in control of events? As he half turns his face becomes a mask of intense concentration. He psychs himself with a quick burst of 'self-talk', to focus himself absolutely on what he must do. He then turns back to face the ball. He walks backwards, staring intently at it, and then finally shifts his attention to Shevchenko. The latter reveals the pressure with two nervous wipes of his palm across the sides of his head, what psychologists call 'leakage symbols'. He is perhaps remembering his miss in the closing minute of extra time, and the negative thoughts pile in. And then he sees Dudek, once more going through the demented jellyfish routine on the line. The outcome is the tamest penalty of all – this from Europe's best striker and the player who had calmly scored AC Milan's winner just two years previously against Juventus. Dudek scarcely has to dive and dismissively swats away the ball, which had been hit without pace or conviction straight down the centre.

What Liverpool had won, in addition to their fifth European Cup, was a titanic battle of wills, first by imposing their game on their opponents in a storming second-half comeback, then by giving a masterly display of the psychology of the penalty shoot-out. In describing these events I have used such phrases as 'arousal', 'focus' and 'self-talk'. These are real constructs, drawn from sports psychology, an important discipline widely used in aiding and enhancing sports performance. Unlike other techniques used in this field, however, there is no straightforward way of fingerprinting a player's mental alertness or well-being at any given instant. Whereas physiological stress can easily be determined by monitoring heart rate continuously under match conditions, and defects in playing technique can be corrected by using high-speed images of players in action, sports psychology by contrast is an empirical science, perhaps the most empirical of all the many disciplines that can be applied to performance improvement in football. It is also a very eclectic one, drawing on a variety of skills and techniques and frequently reliant on questionnaires and surveys to reveal specific insights. But the message is clear, perfectly exemplified by Liverpool's clash with Milan and in many thousands of similar encounters: if teams are closely matched in technical ability and fitness, it is very often mental preparation that tips the balance. Coaches and players ignore the psychological side of the game at their peril.

The Brazilians certainly appreciated this after their traumatic encounter with the Hungarians in Berne in 1954. They had 'lost it' long before their invasion of the Hungarians' dressing room after the match, the running fights and the bottle-wielding. It was argued that a major factor was Hungary's wilful, niggling fouling; this really is the oldest trick in the book, the destruction of the opponents' focus and concentration by forcing skills to be subsumed into petty exchanges and retaliations until any semblance of positive football becomes impossible. When they arrived in Sweden for the 1958 World Cup the Brazilian squad sported something quite novel: a team psychologist, who was ridiculed in the press. One commentator described how he encouraged the players to draw pictures of human beings. The purpose was lost on some observers, who found it amusing that some sketches were quite accomplished while others were little better than matchstick men. It is difficult to know at this distance in time exactly what the objective was, but we can speculate that the motive was to minimise anxiety using a powerful tool called 'imaging'. Just how useful this can be in reducing the stress of performing will be explained later. Let us begin though by looking at one of the most important concepts, 'arousal', and the part it plays in competitive team sport.

No physically demanding task can be carried out without some corresponding degree of physical arousal. Applied to exercise or sport generally, this means a combined physiological and mental alertness. As we have seen, there is no simple test that can instantly reveal this important state of competition readiness in a player. Suppose there were, however, and we had a meter that gave a simple read-out. It would be calibrated on a scale ranging from zero, representing complete inactivity such as deep sleep, through moderate wakefulness to its most extreme reading representing intense excitement, even fear. This spectrum of feelings would be accompanied by corresponding levels of anxiety; these would be barely perceptible for low arousal, rising to acute and possibly threatening levels when the physical task seemed difficult to accomplish or dangerous. This underlines an important point: arousal in itself does not trigger anxiety. The response occurs when the subject has made some assessment of the task and weighed it against the skills and preparedness that can be marshalled to carry it out successfully.

If anxiety, sporting or otherwise, persists to the point where it becomes regular or even chronic we then speak about stress, not a good motivator in producing peak performance in any challenging activity. Not all anxious reactions are undesirable, however; even elite athletes experience the sensation and at the right levels such stimuli are an important component of the arousal process itself. The secret lies in keeping things under control; as someone once aptly put it, it is not a question of having butterflies in the stomach, but getting them flying in formation.

Anxiety and the associated physiological responses are classified as *somatic* and *cognitive*. Somatic anxiety (from the Greek, *soma* = the body) is the direct physiological response to the specific arousal, whereas cognitive anxiety is associated with negative or threatening thoughts about the task itself. Studies show that both types increase before a demanding sporting event, although somatic anxiety drops sharply once the activity is under way. By contrast, cognitive anxiety continues throughout the actual competition, fluctuating in response to specific phases of the play. Thus, in the Liverpool–Milan game, cognitive anxiety and its symptoms would have worked on both teams as the game ebbed and flowed in normal and extra time, but would have become hard to suppress when the drama of the shoot-out began.

As already noted there is no 'arousal meter' to detect this state or the associated anxiety. There are certainly physiological responses, including heightened blood pressure, fast breathing, increased heart rate, sweating and elevated levels of certain hormones of which adrenaline is characteristic. All can be measured precisely, but not in a match context, so sports psychologists have generally resorted to carefully defined questionnaires, pre- and post-competition, to evaluate this condition. There are admitted difficulties with these approaches since they cannot be used during the twists and turns of actual competition. And to be scientifically useful, questionnaires must address just those specifics that will give clear and unambiguous insights into the subject's behaviour patterns, and subjects must report faithfully and honestly. Accepting that all this can be achieved, such assessments reveal much about the relationship between arousal and the important response, physical performance.

The classical explanation was developed in the early 1940s and is called 'drive theory'. In its simplest form this assumes that performance is directly proportional to the level of arousal. For routine activity (a simple skill task) the performance would be expected to improve as arousal increased, much like that shown in Fig. 5.1. This simple model goes some way to explaining why experienced performers do better than novices: as pressure increases, or as the task becomes more technically demanding,

Performance

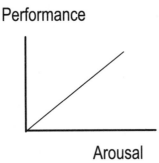

Arousal

Fig. 5.1: Simple drive theory

less experienced players simply make more mistakes and so performance drops away. It was quickly appreciated that this model had limited application, however. For example, even elite players find it impossible to stretch their performances indefinitely and so presumably output must peak at some point, then decline. Psychologists began to think in terms of a model that reflected this – Fig. 5.2 – often referred to as the 'inverted-U' model for obvious reasons. It argues for an optimum level of arousal, beyond which a kind of law of diminishing returns begins to operate. Performance declines even though arousal may go on increasing beyond this point, and the problem for team psychologists or coaches is to find just the right level of arousal for a given player performing a specific skill. This would not be the

Performance
Peak arousal

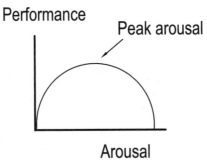

Arousal

Fig. 5.2: 'Inverted-U' model

Performance

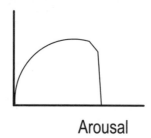

Arousal

Fig. 5.3: Catastrophe theory (after Fazey and Hardy)

same for all players and all physical demands; for example, the degree of arousal for a midfielder making a 20-metre sprint finishing with a winning tackle is not the same as the focused concentration necessary to convert a penalty or free kick. Too much arousal, as Dudek's antics provoked in some of the Milan players, is counter-productive and a price is paid in terms of declining performance. If arousal extends much beyond the optimum, far worse may follow (Fig. 5.3). The subject then enters a regime where even a very small further increase in arousal produces not a gradual downturn but a crash-dive in performance. Psychologists refer to this as 'catastrophe theory', more colloquially as 'choking', and beyond a certain limit subjects are often incapable of any recovery at all. This was evident in marathon-runner Paula Radcliffe's failure in the 2004 Olympic Games, where the enormity of the task and her inability to generate any further output led to the inevitable consequences and her breakdown.

Before looking at measures designed to reduce the destructive effects of arousal-induced anxiety it is important to focus on the individual, since anxiety is very strongly related to personality. The earliest attempts to measure this used questionnaires such as that developed by Eysenck. In its earliest format this measured personality in terms of just two traits: extraversion and neuroticism. Extraverts are outward-going, attention-seeking personalities. Neurotics exhibit high degrees of anxiety. For both traits there are

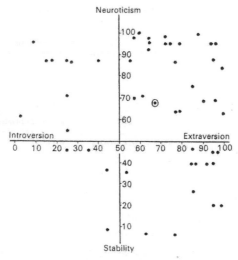

Fig. 5.4: Personality profiles for Australian Rules footballers
(after Davey)

the opposite tendencies: introversion for extraversion and stability for neuroticism.

When tested using Eysenck's Personality Questionnaire (EPQ), athletes can be graphed on diagrams like Fig. 5.4. This is actually a real assessment (Davey, 1987) for an Australian Rules football team, a body of performers not known for timidity in their play. Each marked point on the graph represents an individual player in the squad. The results are revealing in that the team overall exhibits neurotic–extravert tendencies. Average anxiety for the players was rated 70 and extraversion 65, each assessed on a scale from 0 to 100. Australian Rules players as a class have been monitored for over a decade with average scores of 60 in both categories, so the measured team displayed significantly greater than average anxiety. In fact this team regularly failed in senior competition when over-anxiety inhibited their performance. Winning teams by contrast rated 50–55 on the anxiety–extraversion assessment in the EPQ, levels considerably below those of the measured group in Fig. 5.4.

There are many other tests for anxiety assessment in team and individual sports, such as the SCAT (sport competition anxiety test) or the POMS (profile of mood states) tests. While it is dangerous to attempt to extrapolate sporting success from personality tests such as these, there is no doubt that over-anxiety inhibits performance and that some means of reducing it would be beneficial in competition. Any such interventions must address the fact that there is no standard personality, however. Reference to Fig. 5.4 shows that a significant proportion of the subjects tested presented introversion and anxiety to some degree. While it is probably true that a team of introverted neurotics would be unlikely to sweep all before them, it does not mean that these traits, in individual cases, cannot be positively addressed. The problem for coaches is that introverted, anxious subjects tend to reach peak arousal earlier and with far less stimulation than their counterparts. Conversely, they may need more intervention in terms of calming and refocusing when the effects of over-arousal begin to become detrimental to performance.

Promoting initial arousal is not usually a great problem in practice. Generally, a committed, physical workout of around five minutes' duration will achieve the required state and extreme methods are not really necessary. These have ranged in the past from loud, inspirational music, through emotional exhortations from managers and coaches, to tongue lashings and denigration of opponents. At least one highly successful English Premiership manager resorts to the 'hairdryer', a kind of nose-to-nose encounter between drill sergeant and rookie with expectations bellowed out at full volume.

Intervention when anxiety has reached potentially damaging levels can be much more difficult to achieve and it must always be borne in mind that it may be the players themselves who are required to self-administer the remedy. This can be difficult – we are not always the best judges of our own psychological state – so it may take much learning and practice before techniques can be applied during intense competition. There are several effective methods that can be applied, however, notably goal-setting, relaxation, imagery and self-talk.

Goal-setting is widely practised in sport and in many fields of management. At its most fundamental it aims to break complex, daunting tasks into manageable components, thereby reducing the associated stress. In sport, and especially from the player's perspective, it is vital to differentiate between performance and outcome goals. The latter are usually defined in terms of win/lose criteria and can be demotivating for individuals, as they are seldom under a single player's control: how could anyone set a personal goal of winning a given match, or lifting the World Cup? In chasing outcome goals, individuals may have worked with intense commitment, significantly improving personal performance in the process. Failure then becomes extremely demotivating, leading to a downward spiral of doubt, anxiety and further failure.

Performance goals, by comparison, *are* achievable; for example, a player may set a personal target to improve his penalty conversion rate in practice from 50 per cent to 75 per cent over a specific period. There are two important benefits of such a process. Technical skill and confidence both grow in meeting the required performance improvement so players are less likely to choke when the real-life situation comes along. Coaches often refer to the 'staircase' model in performance goal-setting. Individual steps represent the subtasks, and players achieve the desired objective in a steady, controlled climb. The method is very beneficial in reducing somatic anxiety because both technique and confidence are strongly reinforced by following this incremental process.

Relaxation methods to overcome anxiety are of two types: 'centring' and 'progressive muscle relaxation'. Both have the important objective of reducing arousal-related anxiety by lowering muscle tension, heart rate and rapid breathing. In centring, breathing is focused on the abdomen, which is roughly where the human centre of gravity is located. The act of centring focuses the mind on a specific objective, away from negative, distracting thoughts. There is also positive reinforcement in the sense that focus on the centre of gravity emphasises controlled body movements. In centring, individuals operate a breathing cycle of the form: breathe in → breathe out → centre → relax. The sequence may finish with a mental prompt to focus attention on the skill to be performed, while the player remains centred. Progressive muscle relaxation (PMR) is a more comprehensive process that involves alternately tensing then relaxing major muscle groups. Tension is progressively reduced because muscles tend to 'overshoot', relaxing below the starting level after the deliberate contraction is removed. PMR can be valuable if centring alone is insufficient to reduce anxiety, although both methods require significant learning and practice before they can be applied spontaneously in actual competition.

Imagery, where subjects produce a realistic mental picture of the actions they wish to perform, is one of the most powerful techniques in the psychology of performance improvement in sport. It has the enormous benefit of desensitising the activity, in other words of allowing players to practise a skill where perceptions of inadequacy or failure simply do not enter the equation. Mental rehearsal is also thought to stimulate the nervous system and muscles in much the same way as fulfilling the actual task; the term 'muscle memory' has been coined to describe the process. But if mental rehearsal is to be effective it must be as vivid and realistic as the skill itself. The technique works best with discrete activities where some self-contained action is intended; it would obviously be impossible, in any case, to mentally rehearse the myriad individual processes in a complete game. To develop the techniques, subjects often begin with one of the relaxation methods just described. Then the intended skill, with all the essential components, is visualised, both from the inside – seeing all the actions as they would appear through one's own eyes – and from the outside – just as an observer would see the player performing them. Imagery can be combined powerfully with memory recall, especially where a move or action has been perfectly executed at some time in the past. Further imprinting is possible if film or video of this actual event is available. The technique is especially useful in set pieces such as free kicks and penalties as there is usually time to use one of the stress-reduction methods followed by a quick mental replay of the desired actions in these cases.

Self-talk, another method to influence the state of mind of the player, works on personal feelings that are the triggers for behaviour and action, but to be effective, self-talk must be positive. Even what appears to be motivational thinking can result in anxiety and failure if the wrong emphasis is stressed. For example, Shevchenko may have arrived for his penalty full of apparently positive thoughts along the lines of 'If I score, then we make Liverpool play their penalty, and if they miss, we're back in it!' His mental focus becomes locked on not missing his penalty, rather than the positive intention of scoring. The image of failing becomes the dominant one, despite his best intentions, and that is the behavioural response he produces. He could have thought on that long walk from the centre circle, 'Hit the ball to the right, shoulder height, inside the angle,' visualised it, and just before starting his run repeated to himself, 'Right, shoulder, angle.' Practically any positive, affirmative statement concerning an impending action is better than dwelling on negatives and the implications of failure. But to be most effective, self-talk should not be impromptu but carefully built up from previous experience and matched to the specific situations that are faced regularly. The technique is especially good at restoring focus or attention during decisive moments: for defenders in marking up in dangerous set pieces and for the striker who's just about to deliver a demanding free kick.

All of these techniques are designed to hold or restore that critical level of arousal that enables players to produce the goods under pressure, that important feeling of flow or momentum where everything is under control and nothing seems impossible. But as we have seen, opponents are not bound to go along with the plan. If they can impair performance by shaking an opposition out of that comfortable frame of mind, preferably within the framework of the rules, they will. The most noticeable feature of the last decade, though, is how this tactic has spread from the players and the pitch to the media, and with how much relish these mind games are played among the coaching echelons.

It starts in a very familiar format. Team B is an up-and-coming side challenging top-dogs, Team A, for the league title. Coach B modestly announces publicly, 'We are nowhere near good enough to threaten Team A for the title this season.' This undergoes subtle changes in the media when Team B's abilities are compared with Team A's, and Coach A is asked to comment. His remarks are predictably bland, but the message has now subtly changed: Team B is not good enough and Coach A agrees. An outraged Coach B rushes into the dressing room before the crunch game with Team A. 'Look at this,' he shouts, 'they say we're not good enough – we'll show them!' And so Team B is positively motivated by their own coach's initially negative assessment of their abilities. Perhaps Team B opens up a significant lead in the title race. Or perhaps it is a case of Team B competing in several major competitions, or going for a record-breaking run of winning matches. Coach A now has to intervene. 'It's tough when you're in this position,' he declares. 'We've been there and we know how easy it is to blow it when the pressure is on.' What happens next depends very much on the mental toughness of Coach B.

A good example of this – by no means unique – occurred during the 1996 English League Championship race. Newcastle United had built up an impressive points lead on Manchester United and seemed home and dry, until Alex Ferguson began to bait Newcastle manager Kevin Keegan. According to Ferguson, Newcastle owed their position to the fact that teams tried harder against Manchester than against Newcastle. This ludicrous statement should have been laughed off, along with other equally ridiculous assertions by the canny Scot that referees regularly failed to award penalties in United's favour, insufficient time was added on for stoppages at the end of their games, and so on. All good knockabout fun, but Keegan swallowed the bait. Following a game in which Newcastle won a closely contested match with Leeds United, he imploded on national television, and with a voice choking with emotion said, 'I think you have to send a tape of this game to Alex Ferguson – isn't that [Leeds' performance] what he wants? You just don't say that about Leeds. I would love it if we could beat them. He's gone down a lot in my estimation . . . I would love it if we beat them. Love it.' Those little 'ifs' are the give-away, the tips of a massive iceberg of doubt – and probably sealed Newcastle's fate. If a coach cannot project personal confidence, how can he motivate a team? Newcastle were overhauled by Manchester United and finished second to them in the title race in 1996.

Not all coaches succumb to the treatment though. Arsène Wenger of Arsenal has, like Keegan, been on the receiving end of Ferguson's destabilising tactics, but, unlike Keegan, managed to retain his balance, often returning Ferguson's barbs with interest. When, after a premature exit from the Champions League in 2002 Ferguson stated that his side had been the best team in the English Premiership since the Christmas just gone, Wenger quipped, 'Everyone thinks they have the prettiest wife at home.' This rather gnomic comment silenced the Scot, and perhaps this is the best way to 'return service' in the mind game, simply to give as good as one gets.

Psychological interplays are equally revealing in helping us to understand a much darker side to football, when violent acts occur. The very worst incidents relate to football hooliganism. Just three of very many examples give an indication of how far this kind of behaviour has permeated football and how peripherally the actions sometimes relate to the game itself.

The first concerns the Heysel Stadium tragedy on 29 May 1985, when 39 lives were lost following a charge on Juventus fans by Liverpool supporters, the two groups having been poorly segregated in the same part of the ground. The second violent incident concerns the confrontation between Ajax and Feyenoord supporters in March 1997. It was only nominally connected with a game of football. Dutch police were following a contingent of Feyenoord's fans to their game, but expected a violent confrontation with supporters of Ajax at some point during the journey. Ajax, incidentally, were not playing Feyenoord in their game that day. The hooligans, numbering more than 100, abandoned their cars on a motorway, crossed to a prearranged site and began to fight the assembled Ajax fans with steel rods, hammers, bats and chains. One person was killed and there were numerous serious injuries. The final example occurred on 9 June 2002 in Moscow, over 5,000 miles from the game that was being played. Fans were watching the World Cup match between Russia and Japan on a large outdoor screen near Red Square. Russia lost and the spectators, exclusively Russian as far as is known, rioted. Two people died and 50 were seriously injured. These are extreme cases, but many similar examples, exhibiting varying degrees of violent conduct, could be quoted from almost every location in the world where the professional game is played.

Then there is whole-team violence, fortunately now relatively rare. Examples include the running fights between Brazil and Hungary at the 1954 World Cup in Switzerland and the reprise when Italy and Chile slugged it out in the 1962 World Cup match in Santiago. In the middle 1960s, the players of Leeds United, a team known throughout Europe for the robustness of its play, were sent off twice, en masse, with their opponents to allow tempers to cool.

Individual incidents on the field, those punishable under the rules defining violent conduct, probably account for the largest number of such actions in the game although these do not approach hooligan violence in severity. Nevertheless there have been some spectacular and ugly examples. On 25 January 1995, after being sent off in the game against Crystal Palace, Eric Cantona of Manchester United launched himself Kung-fu style at a spectator who had walked to the front of the crowd to remonstrate with him. On-pitch violence is common. The worst incident in many years occurred in April 2001 when Roy Keane of Manchester United injured Alf-Inge Haaland of Manchester City in a brutal, two-footed lunge. The offence was admitted by Keane in his autobiography and in interviews he expressed no remorse, indicating that he would do it again under the same circumstances.

Nor are managers immune. In January 1989 the late Brian Clough struck a spectator under the spotlight of the BBC's television cameras, so incensed was he following a pitch invasion by the fans. The most famous incident of all, however, occurred on 15 February 2003 when Sir Alex Ferguson admitted to kicking a boot in the Manchester United dressing room, splitting David Beckham's eyebrow in the process.

Finally, there is what could be called 'sanctioned violence', where the level of aggression varies from sport to sport and where its severity is effectively limited by the rules of the individual games. In this respect, violence in Association football scarcely ever reaches the levels experienced in overt contact sports such as American or rugby football. How far players are prepared to go in the Association game depends on their willingness to abide by the rules and the thoroughness with which these are applied by the controlling officials. Rules should be absolutes but cultures in football differ and the strains frequently show when Latin and Anglo-Saxon temperaments collide in international competition.

In thinking of violence in sport generally it would be natural to explore it in terms of some of the concepts already discussed, in terms of arousal for example. But given that arousal would presumably need to be extreme before a violent act could be performed, why shouldn't catastrophe theory – the factor that effectively inhibits action when arousal has passed its peak – kick in to modify, possibly limit, the action, as it does in conventional competition? Perhaps it does, in the sense that many kinds of violence correspond simply to a blind 'lashing out' with little specific purpose in mind, so extreme over-arousal makes the action less clinical in its application than it would otherwise be. This is in contrast with sanctioned violence, in boxing for example, which is quite specific in its purpose. In fact, arousal does play a part in violence in sport, but in combination with other emotional states. The psychological model developed to explain human motivation in this regard is called 'reversal theory' and it can be used to interpret the various violent actions described above.

Reversal theory identifies four emotional states, each of which

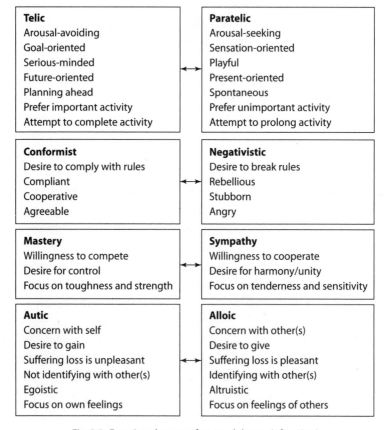

Telic	**Paratelic**
Arousal-avoiding	Arousal-seeking
Goal-oriented	Sensation-oriented
Serious-minded	Playful
Future-oriented	Present-oriented
Planning ahead	Spontaneous
Prefer important activity	Prefer unimportant activity
Attempt to complete activity	Attempt to prolong activity

Conformist	**Negativistic**
Desire to comply with rules	Desire to break rules
Compliant	Rebellious
Cooperative	Stubborn
Agreeable	Angry

Mastery	**Sympathy**
Willingness to compete	Willingness to cooperate
Desire for control	Desire for harmony/unity
Focus on toughness and strength	Focus on tenderness and sensitivity

Autic	**Alloic**
Concern with self	Concern with other(s)
Desire to gain	Desire to give
Suffering loss is unpleasant	Suffering loss is pleasant
Not identifying with other(s)	Identifying with other(s)
Egoistic	Altruistic
Focus on own feelings	Focus on feelings of others

Fig. 5.5: Emotional states of reversal theory (after Kerr)

has its opposite. Kerr (2005), Apter (1997) and others have identified combinations of emotional states shown in Fig. 5.5 with their descriptions. They are telic – the arousal-avoiding state – and its opposite, paratelic – the arousal-seeking state. The conformity state is paired with its opposite, negativity. The mastery state pairs with sympathy and the autic state with the alloic one. This latter pairing needs a little interpretation. Autic individuals are concerned with the self and focus on individual feelings. Alloic individuals are concerned with the feelings of others. In the normal course of events, footballers exhibit conformist tendencies (playing to the rules, getting on with the game) unless reversals are initiated. These are thought to be involuntary and triggered by external events rather than personal choice. Thus a player may be driven from a conformist state into its opposite, a negativistic one, by being directly fouled, or seeing a team mate roughly treated by the opposition. Negativism in this context does not mean indifference; it connotes rebelliousness and anger as motivating characteristics.

Certain combinations of the emotional states ultimately promote violence. These combinations are shown in Fig. 5.6 and lead to outcomes that these researchers classify as anger violence, thrill violence, power violence and play violence, which can help us to understand the various incidents described above, from hooliganism to dressing-room spats.

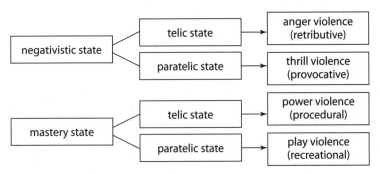

Fig. 5.6: Emotional state combinations producing violence (after Apter)

Anger violence prompted the running fights involving the teams in the World Cup matches in Switzerland and Chile, and also accounts for Eric Cantona's outburst at Crystal Palace, leading to his assault on a spectator. In anger violence the reversal is from the conformist state to the negativistic one and the action is almost always justified by the perpetrator(s) as retaliation, whether in response to provocation or injury to oneself or to a team mate. Because individuals, initially at least, are not arousal-seeking in this state the violent act is usually a sufficient release and matters would normally end at that point. The perpetrator may even reverse once more into the conformist state with no further violent intent. However, the prime instigator, the person who prompted the initial retaliation, is now a victim in turn, and so the cycle of violence escalates, possibly spreading throughout the team unless it is contained. This was very much the pattern in the Cantona incident; his sending-off was prompted by a violent tackle on his part (revenge). Cantona is then abused by a spectator (becomes victim). He launches his celebrated kick (revenge). The spectator throws a punch and Cantona (again victim) retaliates (revenge). Cantona's team mates, Paul Ince and others, were also involved before Cantona was restrained, so the incident had all the latent characteristics of team violence, which might have escalated further involving confrontation with other spectators in the vicinity.

Thrill violence is at the root of most football hooliganism, although it can rapidly degenerate to anger violence with much more serious consequences. Individuals in this state exhibit negativity combined with arousal-seeking behaviour. The negativistic state promotes rule-breaking and provocative acts. The reversal occurs from the conformist state and may be prompted by feelings of boredom or triggered by the need for greater levels of felt arousal. Reversal from conformity to the negativistic state can also be stimulated by small groups – the hooligan ringleaders – who are purposely bent on violence and act as catalysts for the majority. Before giving expression to violent acts the perpetrators must feel some sort of protective framework which separates them from authority or the consequences of their actions. This is ensured by isolation on the terraces or physical anonymity and detachment from the authorities when running skirmishes occur outside football grounds. All of these characteristics were in evidence at the Heysel tragedy where a limited, ill-equipped police force failed to stamp down on the initial, relatively innocuous exchanges between rival fans located in the same part of the ground. It was significant also that the brutal encounter between Ajax and Feyenoord supporters began when the police cordon was given the slip, and in Moscow when the hooligans appreciated the inadequacy of the policing of the original televised event. There must, of course, be a further heightening of the process before purely thrill violence – a sense of breaking the rules or cocking a snook at authority – escalates to the level where lives are threatened. At that point the process has degenerated into anger violence, where actions are retributive and linked with real or perceived hostilities or retaliations by the other side.

Power violence derives from a reversal from the sympathetic to the mastery state, a characteristic of which is the desire to control and a willingness to compete. Power violence usually combines the mastery state with arousal avoidance. For this apparent contradiction to prevail, and for individuals to produce violent acts routinely, this combination must have been in operation for a prolonged period. There is no sudden reversal of states, as there is in the case of anger violence, for example (conformist to negativistic). The exercise of power violence then becomes accepted as a 'normal' response in what is really a prevailing climate of fear and aggression. These may have been the ruling emotions in the famous dressing-room incident at Old Trafford when Sir Alex Ferguson launched a boot at David Beckham. Ferguson referred to this as a 'freakish accident', but Beckham had to be restrained by team mates, enraged by both the flying boot and the fact that Ferguson had blamed him for the poor performance against Arsenal in the FA Cup game played that day. Was this classic anger violence or a symptom of power violence, reflective of an ingrained management culture? Supporting the latter view is the long history of players who have crossed swords with the master and left the club. These include Paul McGrath, Norman Whiteside, Paul Ince and Jaap Stam. The latter had the temerity to criticise Ferguson in his autobiography and was promptly off-loaded to Lazio football club. Five months after the boot incident, two of which overlapped the close season, Beckham followed the familiar pattern and left for Real Madrid.

Can such a management culture imbue players with the same mentality? Many have seen Roy Keane's infamous tackle on Alf-Inge Haaland as classic anger violence, revenge for an earlier incident between the players. It is really the time that elapsed between the events (three years) and Keane's burning intention to 'get even' that give the lie to this and mark the incident as one of an exercise of power violence. The matter was succinctly stated in Keane's ghosted autobiography: 'I'd waited almost 180 minutes for Alfie, three years if you looked at it another way. I'd waited long enough. I hit him hard. The ball was there (I think). Take that.' Roy Keane has been tipped as a likely successor to Sir Alex Ferguson when each, metaphorically speaking, hangs up his boots.

Play violence, the fourth type of hostile action, is achieved when reversal to the mastery state is combined with arousal-seeking behaviour. Like thrill violence, this condition requires a protective frame in order to operate; this is provided by the game rules themselves and the officials who administer them. If the game is to be enjoyed by the participants there must be agreement that the rules, by and large, will be observed, so the state, in addition to the mastery, arousal-seeking combination shown in Fig. 5.6 must also include a high degree of conformist, rather than negativistic tendencies. Applied to Association football the expression 'sanctioned violence' in relation to normal play is a relative one, and in this context will not involve the degree of physical violence tolerated in American football, rugby or ice hockey, for example. Nevertheless, physical contact has not been entirely eliminated in the Association game. Fair shoulder charges are still permitted when the ball is within playing distance and the contenders are genuinely trying to reach it. This is why 'violence' such as shoulder charging or robust tackling can be interpreted as fair play on occasion, even when northern and Latin temperaments clash on the field.

As already noted, sports psychology is an empirical science, very eclectic in terms of the individual insights and methods it can bring to bear on performance improvement in sport. We can validly question how deeply such techniques have penetrated the professional game and how sports psychologists are currently valued in terms of potential contribution. There has been little quantitative research enabling international, even European, comparisons to be made, but one important study has been carried out regarding such perceptions in the English game. In 2004 Matthew Pain and Chris Harwood undertook a detailed survey of knowledge and attitudes among an elite group numbering 56 individuals, comprising national coaches, youth academy directors and academy coaches. The study was prompted by the FA's decision to introduce a 'Psychology for Football' strategy, a positive and forward-looking initiative intended to develop better players and coaches in England.

Pain and Harwood adopted a two-pronged approach. They first circulated a detailed questionnaire to the academies (there were, in 2004, 38 such institutions) and to 11 national coaches. The response rates were 55 per cent from the academies and 73 per cent from the national coaches. Questions were structured using the familiar 5-point Likert scale, along the lines 'Mark the number that represents the knowledge you have of the following topics'. A rating of '1' represented no knowledge, '3' fair knowledge and '5' excellent knowledge of the topic. In terms of the psychological concepts that have been discussed so far, the 56 individuals in the survey produced average scores for knowledge rating as follows. Goal-setting was best understood and rated

3.74, better than 'fair', but not quite 'good'. Imagery/visualisation came out at 3.04, rating 'fair'. Self-talk and relaxation rated 2.74 and 2.4, worse than 'fair' but not quite 'none at all'.

A similar rating system was used to assess the perceived barriers to entry for sports psychology consultants wishing to work alongside the professional staff in the national game. The most significant barrier was considered to be finance; curious in the sense that the cost of employing such people would probably not amount to even a couple of weeks' wages for average players in the English Premiership.

But it was the verbatim comments recorded in the follow-up interviews that were most revealing. In interpreting these one must be aware of the findings of earlier studies, where negative perceptions of sports psychologists were linked to the view, among some coaches and managers, that the discipline was associated with vulnerabilities and weakness, with problem athletes in other words. Thus one academy director stated, 'I still think some people fight shy of the word "psychology". They'll have people working in the clubs but they're loath to admit that they're sport psychologists. They'll call them a coach or a mentor or something like that. So there's some people very aware that they could be ridiculed if they call them sport psychologists, but they will encompass them under a different name. The term "psychologist" is becoming more accepted in football, but is not fully accepted as yet. We do use psychology but we don't call it that. We dress it up. It would be difficult employing a sports psychologist here, named as such.'

Pain and Harwood conclude by recognising that 'Knowledge of sports psychology was limited amongst the majority of those surveyed' but end on an upbeat note: 'If the FA's psychology strategy can deliver the appropriate education to the football community in England, and if consultants can continue to demonstrate their worth within the challenging culture of soccer, the barriers will begin to be overcome.'

Way to go, as our American cousins would put it.

CHAPTER 6

BACK TO BASICS – KICKS, HEADERS AND THROWS

Mental toughness and the ability to handle mind games are important attributes in modern football. The complete player will need an overlay of many more competencies, however: the will to run and tackle and to support others in a disciplined playing formation, and the ability to bring the carefully rehearsed moves of the training ground to the key set pieces the game offers up from time to time, where victory can be won or thrown away in a flash. The greatest players have these skills in abundance but anyone who aspires to be a footballer must master the basics and be able to kick, head and throw the ball well. Detailed match analysis produced the surprising finding that any individual player is in contact with the ball for only 2 per cent of the total distance he covers in a game, so the opportunity to display these skills may seem limited. That is the great paradox of football. These limited touches ultimately decide matches and it is not surprising that much research is devoted to the three basic skills of kicking, heading and throwing.

The ball is the fourth vital ingredient, and it too has become more sophisticated in line with the developing game. The modern version bears little resemblance to the token objects used in the violent mob games of the Middle Ages. These were often crude leather cases stuffed with straw or wood shavings, designed to be mostly carried rather than kicked. Inflated animal bladders were also popular around this time but their fragility limited their use to simpler games and not until they were encased in leather for protection could they be used in serious play. The transition to something resembling the modern ball was gradual, but by the middle nineteenth century leather-cased balls with regular stitched panels had made an appearance. A lighter, inflated ball was obviously much more receptive to kicking than the medieval object, but not until the 1960s did synthetic materials replace natural leather for the casing and solve one of football's most annoying problems – the ball's tendency to absorb water, with a corresponding increase in weight.

The modern ball is a complex structure. Individual polymer panels are still stitched to form the casing (carcass in modern terminology) or, increasingly, thermally bonded to produce a continuous, impermeable surface. Below this is a thin microcellular layer composed of minute gas bubbles, designed to ensure that the impulse of a kick or header is transmitted evenly to the ball. Below this again is a textile mesh that ensures that the ball deforms uniformly in the impact zone and, equally important, recovers and retains its sphericity in flight. And finally comes the latex bladder, inflated both to provide the perfect spherical shape and to ensure consistent recoil in a bounce, header or kick. Surprisingly, despite huge technological input, there is still controversy when a new ball for a major tournament is selected. Diameter and weight are carefully controlled within fixed limits, but the modern tendency is for the weight to be closer to the upper limit, with the diameter correspondingly nearer to the lower permitted value. A heavier, slightly smaller ball produces a truer trajectory as it is less susceptible to random aerodynamic effects in flight. For the players the questions are more pragmatic: is the swerve predictable and can the ball be passed long distances with confidence? Goalkeepers, fearful of unpredictable movements, naturally never see things from the same perspective as elite free-kickers, who want a ball that is fast in flight but capable of producing a controlled swerve. Choice of the specific supplier for a major tournament, for example the World Cup, falls to the game's authorities such as FIFA, but manufacturers naturally like to gain acceptability for their products and will often evaluate prototype designs by gauging player reactions in informal trials.

The most fundamental property of a football is its bounce. Dropped vertically on to a hard surface it recoils, but never to quite the original height. The quantity that determines the strength of the recoil is called, in physics, the coefficient of restitution, e. It is the ratio of the velocity (speed) of the ball immediately after impact to the velocity before. Footballs dropped on to a hard surface give e-values typically around 0.8. Perfect recoil would give a value of 1 and no speed would be lost in the impact, an example of perfect elasticity. Conversely, a ball landing in a muddy, churned-up penalty area often scarcely bounces at all and the e-value would be close to zero. Recoil, and the e-value, depends both on the ball and the surface. When a ball is kicked or headed or bounces from the pitch it distorts during the contact phase and goes through a very fast sequence of stretching the various layers, from the casing to the bladder, as well as compressing the gas it contains. The surface with which the ball makes contact behaves in a similar way. Not all of the ball's components are completely elastic during the impact phase: the casing, for example, is much less so than the latex bladder, so a proportion of the input energy is lost when the ball recoils, and this is why e-values are always less than 1 in practice.

High ball speed from a kick or header may be the desired outcome but there could be a price to pay in terms of the forces generated during the contact, especially if these are accidental impacts with the head. Just how quickly the head and the brain accelerate determines the severity of the potential injury. Using gravitational acceleration, g, as the standard (one g is the rate at which bodies freely fall to earth), unconsciousness occurs when the brain experiences an acceleration of $80g$ and fatalities occur at $200g$. Deliberate heading is currently thought to be below the

lower injury threshold, although temporary unconsciousness
often results from shots unintentionally blocked by the head at
close range.

Experimental impacts are studied using force plates. These are
really only sophisticated weighing machines but designed with
flat, rigid surfaces, instrumented so that fast transient effects can
be recorded. Rapid sampling times are necessary as the contact
phase when a football impacts and recoils is usually all over in
around 60 milliseconds for a ball bouncing off the pitch and even
more fleeting (around 10 milliseconds) for contact with the foot
in a fast kick.

Fig. 6.1 shows the calculated impact profile for a ball dropped
on to a force plate. The speed just before impact was assumed
to be 20 metres per second, typical of that achieved in a long
throw, but considerably less than that for free kicks, which is
usually in the range of 25–30 metres per second. The peak
force of 720 Newtons (equivalent to the weight of a 73-kg
person) is attained after only 9 milliseconds in a total contact
time of 60 milliseconds. If this kind of force prevailed through-

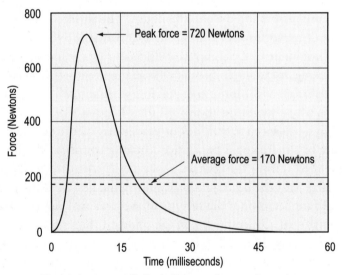

Fig. 6.1: Impact profile for ball dropped on to a force plate

out the whole contact the consequences of heading a ball would be very serious. Fortunately the duration of the peak force is very short and what matters in injury terms, in heading especially, is the 'impulse', defined as the average force acting, multiplied by the contact time. The average force in Fig. 6.1 is 170 Newtons, and would not give rise to injury concerns, particularly in heading. For much greater speeds and certainly for accidental impacts to the head at close range the consequences could be more serious since both peak and average forces rise with impact speed and ball weight.

Because of the need for consistency in performance and safety, FIFA's specification for ball tolerances is exact and covers such properties as weight, size, sphericity, pressure loss, water absorption and recoil. Interestingly, one of the most important properties, the ball's tendency to swerve when kicked with spin, is not regulated. The swerve is determined by two factors: the ball's aerodynamic 'roughness' and the amount of spin that can be produced by the kicker. The former depends on the depth of actual or simulated stitching in the surface panels, the latter on the frictional contact between boot and ball, frequently enhanced by applying frictional surfaces to the instep and side of the boot. Measuring and specifying allowable aerodynamic performance in the ball would not be difficult and might go some way to reconciling strikers' and goalkeepers' ideas about what constitutes the perfect ball in practice.

Under match conditions the ball seldom recoils purely vertically as it does when dropped in a test, and most of the bounces are likely to be at oblique or glancing angles. This can make ball control difficult when the surface conditions are treacherous, for example when the grass is wet and slippery and the pitch is dead, i.e. unresponsive to vertical bounce. On such surfaces the ball often appears to shoot forward on landing. Commentators frequently describe this as the ball 'picking up speed' from the surface. It doesn't actually go faster because it loses energy overall in the impact. What happens is that the ball skids during the very brief contact phase so its horizontal velocity is little altered. If the e-value for the impact is very low, as it will be for soft or water-logged surfaces, there will be scarcely any rebound, so after impact the horizontal velocity dominates, giving the impression of increased forward speed. For many years artificial pitches were not accepted because of their unrealistic recoil properties, although it was their excessive liveliness rather than surface stodginess that caused the problem.

Much of the theory of impact and recoil can be applied to kicking and this is far and away the most intensively studied skill in football. The action has many flavours, from the simple side-foot pass to the full-velocity instep kick. Then there are the subtle variations designed to produce just the right combination of speed and spin in a swerving free kick.

The ball is easiest to control when played at rest from the ground but occasionally it must be hit on the volley – before it bounces – and sometimes on the half-volley – a split second after it has bounced. Both of these actions require great timing and skill and can produce spectacular goals, although little research has been carried out on either for shots from close range. The volley and half-volley are noticeably effective for long-range kicking; goalkeepers often clear the ball this way, the objective being to move it well into the opponents' half of the field. Kicking for distance was studied by McCrudden and Reilly in 1993. It was found that volleys travelled further than half-volleys (40.1 metres as opposed to 36.1 metres), but as the speed at which the ball left the foot and the angle it made with the horizontal were not reported, it remains an open question as to which is the better technique in terms of kicking for distance. There is some thought that goalkeeper clearances using half-volleys allow greater accuracy in the delivery. This seems to be the case from simple eye-witness observations but it is noticeable that, when goalkeepers attempt a long pass to a team mate in this way, the range of the kick is constrained and the trajectory kept deliberately flat.

Both help to minimise the time of flight and reduce the likelihood of an interception.

The basic action of kicking a stationary ball from the ground brings us back to the question of impact and exactly what goes on in the very fleeting contact between the foot and the ball. Essentially, it is a very fast two-stage process. Kinetic energy – the energy associated with a moving object's speed – is stored in the kicking leg as it swings down into contact with the ball. This energy is transferred briefly as internal energy when the ball is compressed during the impact and is released as kinetic energy once more when the ball leaves the foot and recovers its shape. For the moment let us ignore spin effects and see how this energy transfer determines the ball's ultimate velocity in a typical instep kick.

Fig. 6.2: Instep kick (after Lees)

Fig. 6.2 shows the preliminary run-up, kick and follow-through. Also shown (Fig. 6.3) are the angular velocities of the thigh (hip to knee) and shank (knee to ankle) as the movement develops. Angular velocity is simply speed of rotation. The scientific units shown in the figure are radians per second (rad s^{-1}) but they can be expressed in the more familiar form of revolutions per minute (rpm). For example, the peak rotational speed in the figure is about 30 radians per second, equivalent to 286 rpm. Fig. 6.3 shows the progression of the kick in four important stages. Stage 1 represents the backlift as the leg flexes at the knee. In Stage 2 both thigh and shank move rapidly downwards, but whereas the thigh begins to slow

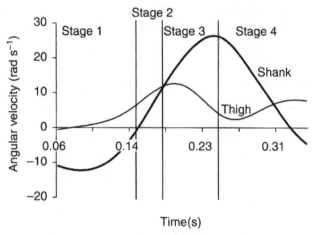

Fig. 6.3: Angular movement of leg in instep kick (after Lees)

down at the end of Stage 2, the shank continues building its rotation speed until it reaches a peak at the end of Stage 3, where contact with the ball occurs. Stage 4 simply represents the follow-through of the kicking leg – thigh and shank – after the ball has gone. The secret of really powerful kicking is not just to achieve the fastest possible rotation of the limbs, but to time the delivery so that this occurs in the instant before contact.

The ball velocity naturally depends on how fast the foot is travelling just before impact, but two other important factors influence the outcome. The first is the *e*-value for the impact which, perhaps surprisingly, works out at about 0.5. This is lower than that usually found for rigid-surface impacts (0.8) because the bones in the foot deform considerably during the contact phase. The second important factor is the ratio of the mass of the kicking leg to that of the ball. It could be argued that this number should really be calculated using the mass of the foot alone; after all, this is the object that actually makes contact with the ball. Roughly speaking the mass of the human foot is about a kilogramme and the ball weighs about half a kilogramme so the ratio would appear to be 2. The value determined by experiment, however, is about 4. This is because in powerful kicking the ankle and knee joints are kept as rigid as possible so some of the mass of the upper leg is factored into the impact. For this reason we often speak of the 'effective' mass of the leg in kicking. Broadly speaking the greater the e-value and the greater the effective mass of the kicking leg, the greater the release velocity of the ball. Using an e-value of 0.5 and a leg/ball mass ratio of 4, a simple equation can be derived showing the relationship between the release speed of the ball and the speed of the kicking foot:

$$v_{release} = 1.2 \cdot v_{foot.}$$

This tells us, perhaps surprisingly, that the ball speed works out to be 20 per cent greater than the speed of the kicking foot. So foot speeds of 21 to 25 metres per second will produce ball speeds of 25 to 30 metres per second, the ideal range for free kick deliveries. If the ball had perfect elasticity ($e = 1$) and the player a hugely massive kicking leg (technically infinite!), then the equation above would change to

$$v_{release} = 2 \cdot v_{foot:}$$

and the ball speed would be exactly twice the kicking speed. Although this theoretical value is unlikely ever to be achieved in practice, there is no doubt that Roberto Carlos' enormous thigh and calf musculature contributed to the ball speed he needed to hammer it nearly 35 metres in his famous scoring free kick against the French in the Tournoi de France in 1997.

Maximal velocity may be important for some shots but more subtlety is required if the ball is to be swerved in flight. This is achieved when spin is applied to the ball by striking it at specific points around the circumference, as shown in Fig. 6.4. Maximum ball speed is produced when the line of the kick passes exactly through the ball's centre of mass, but no spin is produced in this case. Successively greater spin is produced the further the

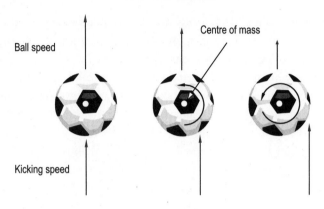

Fig. 6.4: Variable impact point for velocity/spin trade-off

contact point is off-set from the centre of mass, but there's an inevitable trade-off since the speed of the ball declines in the process. Spin can be enhanced with good frictional contact between the boot and the ball and there is now a massive industry dedicated to designing friction surfaces applied to the critical contact areas of the boot.

Perhaps the only other point to make about kicking is the obvious one. Once the ball has left the foot, there's nothing more the striker can do to influence the flight, and aerodynamics takes over. Air resistance now has an added effect on the speed of the ball. Imagine a ball struck with medium power so that it leaves the foot at 25 metres per second. We can calculate how fast it will be travelling after covering various standard distances, such as the distance to the defensive wall, the penalty kick distance, after a 25-metre free kick, a 37-metre corner kick and a 65-metre goal kick. The results are shown in Table 6.1, together with the proportion of the kinetic energy retained after the various distances. Not much speed or kinetic energy is lost until the ball has travelled an appreciable distance. This underlines again the injury potential implicit in accidental contacts with the ball at short range, for example when defending in a defensive wall. Stopping the ball unintentionally with the head for anything closer than a goal or corner kick would not be a good idea.

Table 6.1: Ball velocity and residual kinetic energy (KE) after various shots

Type of shot (Initial speed = 25 metres per second)	Distance (metres)	Final speed (metres per second)	Residual KE (%)
Defensive wall distance	9.1	22.7	82
Penalty kick	11	22.3	80
Free kick	25	19.3	60
Corner kick	37	17.0	46
Goal kick	65	12.7	26

In impact terms heading is very like kicking, and the speed coming off the head depends very much on the ball's arrival speed. Experiments show that the head moves typically between 3 to 5 metres per second in a firm header, clearly much less than the speeds attainable by the foot in instep kicking. To achieve this, however, both the trunk and the neck must be powerfully rotated and the forward speed further enhanced by running and jumping at the ball before impact. If this combination cannot be achieved then the strength of the header will be much reduced, as the neck muscles alone must do all the work. This is often seen when players are forced to head weakly because the timing of the run to the ball has been misjudged or the ball arrives unexpectedly. On the plus side, higher e-values can be achieved in heading, typically around 0.7 compared with 0.5 for kicking, because the neck and shoulder muscles can be braced much more rigidly than the bones of the foot during the crucial contact phase, enabling more of the body's mass to feature in the collision.

The mechanics of heading are more complex than kicking since both the ball and the head are in motion whereas the ball was assumed to be stationary during the kick. Nevertheless an equation can again be derived that relates the strength of the header – the speed at which the ball returns – to the incoming ball speed and the speed of the head:

$$v_{return} = 1.7 \cdot v_{head} + 0.7 \cdot v_{ball.}$$

For a head velocity of 5 metres per second and an incoming ball speed typical of a goal kick of 12.7 metres per second, the return speed of the ball would be 17.4 metres per second. This would ensure a headed clearance of around 25 metres, fairly typical of the distance achieved in a defensive header. If we consider an incoming speed of 17 metres per second typical of a corner kick (or a free kick near the touchline opposite to the penalty area) the return speed of the header would be 20.4 metres per second, getting on towards the pace of a decent shot. The trick with attacking headers from corners and free kicks, however, is to combine a high return speed with a redirection of the ball towards goal. This may entail anything from the finest glancing header to one where the ball is turned through a right angle. Achieving this for a ball swerving in flight under hostile pressure from defenders is no easy task. Nor is there the luxury of a 'first touch' where a striker can kill the ball's pace by bringing it under control before shooting at goal. Small wonder that gifted headers of the ball are prized assets in any team.

The final basic skill in football is the throw, which at first sight may not seem to have much in common with kicking or heading. There is no impact involved in a throw but there is an important build-up where angular rotation in the trunk and arms is eventually released as kinetic energy in the ball. Superficially, the action of throwing is closely related to that of kicking, as the intention is to build up maximum rotation speed in the arms and wrists. In throwing, the wrists – like the foot in kicking – attain peak velocity at the moment of release, whereas the other body segments – the elbow, shoulder and hip – are slowing down. Just as with instep kicking there are several ways to get the ball moving quickly in a throw. Most players favour a run-up at the end of which the ball may be released with the feet planted side by side. However, the longest throwers prefer to place a leading foot in front of the other as more of the momentum generated in the run-up is retained in the ultimate throw. There is a spectacular alternative to these traditional methods capable of producing greater release velocity still. In this, a conventional handspring is used. This is more usually seen in floor exercises in gymnastics where the athlete pivots about the hands, placed firmly on the ground after a short run, eventually landing back on the feet. The movement is identical in a handspring throw in football, but the rotation takes place when the ball, held firmly in the hands, is planted instantaneously on the ground after the run-up. As the whole body is now rotating and not just the upper parts, as in a conventional throw, greater angular momentum is produced.

Studies of this technique (Messier and Brody, 1986) confirmed average release speeds for conventional throwers of 18.1 metres per second compared with 23 metres per second for the handspring throwers. It may be highly effective at getting the ball away quickly, but the technique has not found favour at any level of play in European competition, perhaps because surface conditions around the touchline seldom provide the degree of traction needed to complete the move in safety.

Long throwing is an important technical skill. Elite throwers using conventional methods can easily achieve distances in excess of 40 metres, the world record currently standing at just over 48 metres. Release velocity is perhaps the most important parameter, but it is essential to control the launch angle carefully. The familiar 45-degree release angle for the maximum range of a conventional projectile simply does not apply. In our studies (Bray and Kerwin, 2004) we have found that much shallower release angles are used, typically 36 degrees. This is because aerodynamic forces come into play immediately the ball is released, one of the most important being aerodynamic lift caused by the ball's spin. This is generated by the thrower's wrists in the final phases of the throw. Our studies have shown that a significant amount of backspin, not previously thought to influence long throwing, is produced at release. The rates of ball spin achieved, around 3 revolutions per second (29 rpm), do not compare with the rates generated in free kicks, which are about 3 or 4 times this figure, but they are nevertheless capable of extending the throw by 5 metres or more.

These three basic skills – kicking, heading and throwing – are drawn on repeatedly throughout the course of any game. The actions should always be purposeful, and in an ideal world a pass would always reach a team mate and a defensive header would never return possession to the opposition. Unfortunately life is not like this and it is understandable if defenders occasionally hoof the ball clear simply to relieve attacking pressure, or strikers produce an optimistic snap-shot at goal before defenders close in. There are occasions though when football confers a precious advantage to the attacking side, where ample time is available to execute the perfect shot in a penalty or free kick, or where rehearsed tactics can be brought into play for a corner kick or a long throw. These are the game's set pieces, discussed in the chapter that follows. Whilst it is still possible to miss, fans are much less forgiving of a penalty kick that is fluffed compared with a 30-metre pass that fails to complete; and rightly so, when the chances of scoring in a penalty are so loaded in favour of the striker, as we shall shortly see.

CHAPTER 7

SET PIECES – THE GAMES WITHIN THE GAME

Set pieces are an increasingly important feature of the modern game, accounting for a growing proportion of goals scored in major competitions. Some sources put the figure as high as 40 per cent, others between a quarter and a third. What number you come up with really depends on what you include in the definition. Set pieces are strictly those parts of play that follow on from where the game is started or restarted, possibly after an infringement. This brings some fairly innocuous events into the frame such as the kick-off or the bounce-up, when the referee simply drops the ball between two opposing players. Because goals from such sources are very unlikely, some studies have tended to restrict the definition to throw-ins, corners and free kicks, where the chance of scoring is obviously greater. Sometimes this limited definition is enlarged to include penalties, raising the problem of whether goals scored in a penalty shoot-out should also be included. They should not conventionally be reported in the aggregate score for a match because, technically, the shoot-out is simply the decider for the team that wins a tournament or progresses to the next stage. Nevertheless we frequently read that 'Team A beat Team B, 5–4 on penalties'.

All this is confusing enough, but there is also the issue of how many contacts with the ball should count in the build-up to a goal when defining a set piece. A penalty is almost always resolved in a clean strike, whereas a goal from a corner kick or long throw may follow a combination of headers or passes. How many touches should be allowed before a set piece devolves into continuous play? There really is no convincing answer and the only safe approach is to define the set piece carefully so that any resulting goals can be properly attributed in the statistics.

Table 7.1: Goals scored from set pieces in 1998 World Cup. Total goals were 171 in open play, 191 including penalty shoot-outs

Set piece	Goals scored
Throw-ins	1
Corner kicks	20
Free kicks	21
Penalties (open play)	15
Penalties (shoot-outs)	20

Before looking at the various plays in depth some figures may be helpful. In 1999 Grant, Williams and Reilly analysed goals scored in the 1998 World Cup final. This was won by the host nation, France, in a memorable game in which they beat Brazil 3–0. It was one of those occasions when the Brazilians lapsed into nervous introspection. They needed a penalty shoot-out in the semi-final to see off the Dutch, but had no answer to Zinedine Zidane's power and finishing in the final. There were 171 goals in the 1998 tournament excluding 20 scored in shoot-outs. Grant, Williams and Reilly used a restricted definition of set pieces including only throws, free kicks and corners in their analysis, but in Table 7.1 I have added penalties from both normal play and shoot-outs. Based on the restricted definition, set pieces accounted for 25 per cent of the 171 goals scored. Add penalties from normal play and the figure rises to 33 per cent; it jumps to 40 per cent when penalties from shoot-outs are included in the total. These variations reveal the difficulties of finding a satisfactory definition and underline the need for clarity and consistency, especially when performance comparisons are made.

The findings of Table 7.1 are broadly confirmed from similar assessments. For example, using the narrow definition of set pieces (all penalties excluded), the goals scored in the 1990 and 1994 World Cups were 32 per cent and 25 per cent of the total. World Cup football may not be representative of the game at club level, but the figures do underline the importance of set pieces as a valuable potential source of goals. And given their frequency – about 45 throws, corners and free kicks combined occur, on average, in international games – they can also be planned and practised with confidence. Few teams nowadays, defending or attacking, approach a dangerous set play without some idea of its likely execution.

Table 7.2: Set pieces in football

Set piece	Score with one touch?
Goal kick	Yes
Throw-in	No
Corner kick	Yes
Direct free kick	Yes
Goalkeeper/attacker one-on-one	Yes
Penalty and penalty shoot-out	Yes

The commonly accepted set pieces are the goal kick, throw-in, corner kick, direct free kick, goalkeeper/attacker one-on-one and the penalty and penalty shoot-out, as shown in Table 7.2. Most follow the strict definition of a start or restart of play. The table also indicates those where a goal can legally be scored with one touch of the ball. Excluded are the bounce-up and kick-off, neither likely to make the average fan's list of sensational events. While the bounce-up has zero goal-scoring potential, the same is not true of the kick-off. It cannot be done with a direct shot but it would be possible following a short pass. The only question then is whether the goal can be threatened with a shot from the half-way line. The answer is yes, and we will look at speculative long-range kicking in relation to goal kicks in a moment. For the most part, though, the kick-off is about retaining possession and building confidence by setting up some passing movements, especially in the early stages of the game.

The exception which does not follow the strict 'start or restart' definition is the goalkeeper/attacker one-on-one, mentioned in Chapter 4. Its inclusion as a set piece is really justified by its goal-scoring potential and the speed with which it is executed. Most encounters of this kind are over in a second or so and a goal often results. Other distinctions could be drawn between the set pieces listed in Table 7.2. For example, scoring direct from a throw is illegal and is not very likely with direct attempts from corners or some free kicks, so assists, where the ball is passed to a team mate, are a practical necessity in such cases. This is not so for the other set pieces and, while there is actually nothing wrong in complicating matters by passing to a team mate (even in a penalty kick) where a direct strike would be preferable, for the most part we will look at set pieces as either direct strikes or opportunities to score in the fewest possible touches.

Table 7.2 has been drawn up with an implicit ranking in terms of goal-scoring potential, from goal kicks (low) to penalties (very high). The problem is that only penalties and shoot-outs have been studied in depth. The conversion rate for penalties in open play is 80 per cent, dropping to 75 per cent for shoot-outs. Success rates in other cases are speculative based on subjective observation: so perhaps 60 per cent of goalkeeper/attacker one-on-ones end in a goal, and direct free kicks succeed on 15 per cent of occasions. The conversion rates for corner kicks probably approach those for free kicks, but those for throws appear to be much smaller, and the true figures are unrecorded. Whatever the probability of scoring, as noted earlier, all set pieces should be part of a pre-determined tactical plan and not left to improvisation on the spur of the moment.

Analysing set pieces is not just an academic diversion. In deadlocked games where defences dominate they may be the only way to break the tactical stalemate, and we should expect the proportion of goals from set pieces to rise as coaches and players become more adept at winning these 'games within the game'. It is fortunate for sports analysts that these are very self-contained events taken against the background of the general play. Biomechanical analysis is then possible because the timescales of each move are so short and the intentions of attackers and defenders very specific.

Set plays offer a strategic advantage in addition to their inherent goal-scoring potential. This is because the attacking side can move up in strength, especially for free kicks, corners and long throws, more securely than would be possible in open play. In such cases the opposition will also need to defend in depth, so numerical near-equality of attackers and defenders can be achieved in the central zone of the attacking third of the pitch. This is in sharp contrast to the normal ratio of strikers to defenders in this zone. Pushing too many players forward in open play is dangerous, given the likelihood of a fast counter-attack when possession is lost.

Let us look at set pieces in detail then, starting at the low probability end with goalkeeper clearances. It is sometimes surprising to discover that goals scored by goalkeepers are not that rare. They were very common before 1912, when goalkeepers were allowed to handle the ball anywhere within their own half of the field. Restricting handling to the penalty area makes things more difficult and getting on the score sheet today requires greater adventurousness. Examples abound, however, from goalkeepers who race up-field in the dying seconds of the game to join a corner or free kick, to those who have turned themselves into penalty or free kick specialists. Peter Schmeichel of Manchester United was a good example of the former and José Luis Chilavert, Paraguay's mercurial keeper, has developed a respected reputation for his penalties and swerving free kicks. Sometimes goalkeepers sign up as penalty takers in a shoot-out and it was Ricardo, Portugal's keeper, who scored the final and decisive penalty against England in the quarter-final of Euro 2004. If all this were not enough, many keepers increasingly play a sweeper's role, moving out of the penalty area to clear a through-ball or just far enough up-field to deliver telling passes to their forwards.

Speculating about scoring direct from a goalkeeping clearance brings us down to earth a little. To even remotely think of scoring from a goal kick the ball must be delivered a prodigious distance. On a regulation pitch of around 101 metres' length, the distance from the goal area to the opposing goal line is 95 metres. Let us make the most generous assumptions possible: the kick is delivered at 30 metres per second (67 mph) and the keeper manages to get a high rate of backspin on the ball, say 500 rpm. He also contrives to produce exactly the right launch angle to guarantee maximum range under these conditions.

Fig. 7.1 shows the maximum length achievable for this kick, very nearly 75 metres. The trajectory of the ball's flight was calculated using the mathematical model (Bray and Kerwin, 2003) described in Chapter 3, adapted to the goalkeeper's kicking action. Maximum release velocity combined with backspin is essential in achieving a long carry. It is usually stated in simple ballistics theory – the science of bodies moving freely under gravity – that projectiles should be launched at 45 degrees to the horizontal to achieve maximum range, but to achieve the carry of Fig. 7.1 the launch angle is much smaller, only 18 degrees.

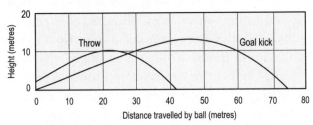

Fig. 7.1: Comparison of long throw and goal kick

This is because simple ballistics ignores air resistance and aero-dynamic lift, both of which modify the trajectory appreciably. The reduced launch angle required for maximum range under real conditions actually works very much in the goalkeeper's favour. Achieving elevations of 45 degrees would be immensely difficult for a ball kicked at speed from the ground.

The carry of 75 metres is substantially more than half the length of the pitch, so, walloping the ball from the centre circle straight after the kick-off could easily reach the goal, but not without a bounce in the case of a goal kick. This is exactly what Spurs' goalkeeper Pat Jennings achieved in the FA Charity Shield match against Manchester United in 1967, when an astonished Alex Stepney watched Jennings' clearance sail over his head after a bounce, into an empty net. What defeated him that day was not just the strength of Jennings' delivery but the assistance provided by a blustery following wind. The model used for Fig. 7.1 can be modified to incorporate wind assistance and it shows that the ball would carry 9 metres further for a following wind of 6.7 metres per second (15 mph). So the message for goalkeepers and coaches is clear: if you fancy a shot, go for it on a really breezy day when the wind is whistling over your shoulder, but do not count on scoring unless you can get the release conditions absolutely right. Perhaps the real message of this set piece is that kicking for extreme length against a well-prepared defence with attackers tightly marked is not very intelligent. The best goal kick is likely to be one that guarantees possession will be retained, even at the expense of extreme delivery distances.

The distance achievable in a long throw is far less than in a goal kick, but long-throwing is steadily becoming a serious attacking option. It may not yet compare with the corner kick or free kick in outright scoring potential, but high accuracy of delivery and throwing speeds exceeding 20 metres per second make it a potent weapon for the game's elite throwers. Most use orthodox throwing rather than the spectacular and potentially longer handspring technique discussed in Chapter 6. There is no question that fans would welcome the occasional exotic delivery, but what professional would take the risk of collapsing in a heap on a slippery winter touchline in front of 60,000 spectators?

The throw itself has undergone some strange transformations since its inception. Under the early rules the first player to get to the ball after it went out of play could take the throw. Because this could be one-handed the ball was often hurled very long distances, much in the manner of over-arm throws used by present-day goalkeepers. Today's rule, with its insistence that the ball be delivered from behind the head with both hands, must have seemed very restrictive initially and it took a long time before technique improved sufficiently for long-throwing to challenge the one-handed feats of the 1870s. While long-throwers can comfortably achieve distances of over 40 metres, routine throw-ins achieve little more than a formal restart to the game, although care will be taken to ensure possession is not surrendered cheaply to the opposition, especially in dangerous attacking positions. It is a different matter when the throw-in can be taken directly opposite to the penalty area. As the half-width of a standard pitch is about 38 yards (35 metres), the far post is just within range for the longest throwers and the near post can easily be reached. As with the corner kick, most goals from throw-ins result from assists at the near post, so all the thrower has to do is attack this position – after a few crucial preparations.

Grip on the ball is essential in really long throwing and, even for a moderate throw, a good rub against the jersey is necessary. For a really polished job, though, the ball is often inserted under the jersey and wiped clean of all mud and moisture. One long-throw specialist used to call for a towel to clean and dry the ball. The rules have nothing to say on the matter and if it produces a spectacular outcome, there seems to be no reason for match officials to be pedantic.

Fig. 7.1 shows the trajectory of a throw that carries 40 metres, sufficient to take the ball into the attacking zones in and around the goal area. To achieve this, just as with long-kicking, the thrower must get the release conditions exactly right, initial elevation and spin especially. It was not widely appreciated how important spin was as a contributory factor in long-throwing, but it was clearly visible in our studies of this technique (Bray and Kerwin, 2004). For this research we used junior professional and good collegiate players as subjects. The best could achieve release speeds just exceeding 18 metres per second, producing optimal throws of around 35 metres. The speed assumed in Fig. 7.1 is 20 metres per second, well within the capability of an elite thrower.

A throw as long as 40 metres has important implications for attackers and defenders alike. Compared with a corner kick that achieves the same distance, the flight time is relatively long: 3 seconds as opposed to 2.1 seconds for the corner. In addition, it is also high, the ball reaching 10 metres at the apex, compared with just over 5 metres for a corner. This gives defenders more time to prepare and, crucially, the goalkeeper has a generally unimpeded view of the ball's flight. Some of the very best throwers try to regain the tactical advantage by throwing with a flatter trajectory. To accomplish this, spin must be increased and yet more speed squeezed out of the delivery, otherwise the ball would not carry the required distance before reaching the ground. Achieving 40 metres with a flat trajectory is difficult, but a lesser distance may still be effective in a flat throw, particularly on a narrow pitch.

The tactics for a long-throw, especially for assists at the near post, are almost identical to those for the corner kick, discussed later. Having said this, corner kicks and long-throws differ in an important aspect. For corners, defenders must stand at least 10 yards (9.1 metres) away, as for a free kick, but until recently there was no such restriction on the defender's positioning for a throw. Unfortunately, elite performers and their throwing styles are very well known, and an effective deterrent was to station a defender very close to the touchline, blocking the intended position of the throw. This prevented an energetic follow-through, essential for all long deliveries, so the run-up necessarily started earlier and finished considerably short of the touchline. Finding space for a long delivery can be difficult on some of the very cramped grounds that still exist even at the top level in today's game. The fact that throwers occasionally deliberately ignored the obstructing defender and finished with the inevitable collision and an ugly confrontation caused the authorities to act. From the 2005–06 season the defender will have to stand 2 metres in-field from the throw. This should promote the long-throw as a valuable attacking option from those positions where the goal can easily be reached.

Another important feature of this set piece is that it is not possible to be offside for a throw. This tactic is sadly under-exploited. If the throw can be quickly taken, it can be used as effectively as a through-ball for a striker running legally beyond the last defenders. The problem is that the first player to the ball may not be the team's best thrower, so the timing of the move is often lost. Most professionals could be coached to improve their throwing effectiveness. If goalkeepers can become dead-ball specialists, outfield players can surely learn a long-throw and play it quickly – it would greatly improve the attacking potential of any side.

Looked at as a direct scoring opportunity, the corner is the least threatening free kick to concede. This is because the goal-face is effectively closed from the kicker's position at the corner flag and to open it up the ball must be played as an in-swinger. The problem in practice is that it is simply not possible to get enough curvature on the kick to swing it very far from the goal line and bring it back in to threaten the target. Our free kick model (Bray and Kerwin, 2003) was used to investigate this set piece. It shows that in all in-swinging corners that result in a goal, the ball is never further than about 2.3 metres from the goal line and, in the important last few metres of its flight, well within the goal area. Further, in this zone it is easily within the jumping reach of a decent keeper. Any such delivery should really be a goalkeeper's gift; it may have been different when forwards could legitimately barge goalkeepers off the ball but this does not apply with the degree of protection they now enjoy. Under today's rules the goalkeeper is (rightly) considered to be 'in possession of the ball' when he is touching it with any part of his hands or arms. Referees interpret this very liberally and there has been a long culture of 'zero contact' as far as continental goalkeepers are concerned.

Given that direct strikes are not too tactically rewarding, attackers in this set piece must look for another approach to result in a score. The prime target for this play, as with the long throw, is the near post, as most goals from corners are scored from assists in this position. This is not to discount opportunities at the far post or deliveries beyond it. Unlike with the long-throw, there is enough power in reserve in a corner kick so that the near or far posts can be attacked with plenty of zip and, equally important, the ball trajectory can be kept low. This is vital in reducing the keeper's visibility of the kick.

Fig. 7.2 shows the classic positions for defenders and attackers in a near-post delivery. The two attackers will in general attract three defenders: one to cover the near post on the goal line and the other two to man-mark the attackers.

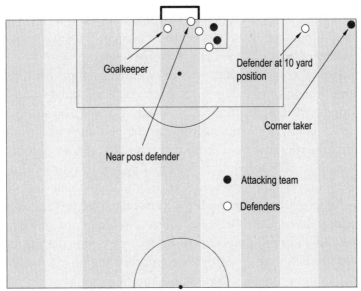

Fig. 7.2: Defending a near-post corner kick

The latter will invariably be good headers of the ball, so they are likely to be covered by one or more of the central defenders. The defending side may additionally station someone at the statutory 10-yard (9.1-metre) point from the corner kick, both to deter the kicker and to prevent a short corner being taken. The attacking side has therefore achieved a very important objective: to draw the defence to a specific point and to deplete it disproportionately elsewhere.

Six players are directly in the goalkeeper's line of sight, so if the corner can be kept low, his view of the ball will be severely impaired. The attackers' job at the near post is simply to move the ball on, by flicking it into the dangerous central zone. As not too much pace will be taken off the ball in a back-header, the defenders face that most difficult challenge: a ball moving quickly across the goal face, amenable to any kind of deflection by attackers or defenders that may see it finish in the net.

Tight in-swingers to the far post should, as already mentioned, be the goalkeeper's property, but there are advantages in attacking the far post zone outside the keeper's reach. If the marking is poor, there are possibilities for a strong header at goal. Equally, the ball may simply be headed back across goal so that a team mate, running in, can attempt a scoring header or shot.

Two other variants of the corner kick are sometimes tried, and both depend on the degree to which defenders can be caught napping. If there is no defender standing at the 10-yard (9.1-metre) point, a shorter delivery can be played to one of the attackers, who runs from the near post position to the edge of the penalty area. This may lead to a shooting opportunity or at the very least to a pass to the corner-taker, who should now have run in-field, improving the angle for an attacking centre. The short corner, played to a colleague at much closer range, has the same intention: to work a more open angle for the centre. Both tactics take valuable seconds and attackers must be alert to the possibilities of being caught offside as their team mates work the ball in-field. Sadly also, defenders are rarely fooled in the top flight and seldom leave attackers unmarked to make runs, medium or short, in this way.

Finally, there is that most curious short corner of all: the ball played to a colleague a metre or so away from the corner flag. In an elaborate twosome this person stops the ball so that the kicker can start again, not far from the original position. About all that can be said is that the accuracy of the kick can be improved since the corner flag is no longer an obstruction. Little is gained, however, either in opening up the attacking angle or shortening the kicking distance, and defences are seldom fooled by this over-elaborate ritual.

Unlike the other set pieces the goalkeeper/attacker one-on-one may involve many touches of the ball before a scoring attempt is made. It starts when the defence has been beaten, leaving a single attacker with a clear run on goal. These encounters can be triggered in many ways: a badly coordinated attempt to play attackers offside, or the interception of a carelessly hit pass by the defence. The dilemma for the goalkeeper can be seen immediately from Fig. 7.3. If he stays on his line, there is a very big target for the striker to shoot at. The assumption is that the goalkeeper can cover a blocking area of roughly 2 metres laterally by 2.5 metres vertically. This is not the 'diving envelope' – the goalie's limit of reach – of a traditional diving save and represents the stretching limits of the limbs without a jump. There is very little time for finesse in these encounters. The operative phrase is 'reflex save' and the goalie will simply try to get *any* part of his anatomy in the way of the shot when it eventually comes. If the goalkeeper leaves his line, he can eventually cover the full goal width (Fig. 7.3), a process known as 'narrowing the angle', for obvious reasons. Technically there is now nothing left for the striker to shoot at, but it is important to remember that goalkeepers are often beaten even in this apparently optimal position. By moving out, the goalkeeper is at least acting decisively, always disconcerting for strikers, and will have improved the chances of a save compared with staying rooted to the goal line.

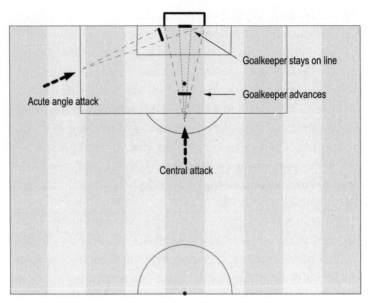

Fig. 7.3: Narrowing the angle in goalkeeper/attacker one-on-one

Fig. 7.3 also shows the position the goalkeeper must reach if the attack comes from a more acute angle. Because the goalface is not as open, it is not necessary to run so far to block the shot. The critical positions can be calculated exactly for any angle of the attacker's approach (Bray, 1972). For example, in a central attack when the striker had reached the edge of the penalty area the keeper would need to be 4.4 yards (4 metres) from the attacker to smother the shot. If the attack came from a more acute angle, say 25 degrees to the goal line, as in Fig. 7.3, the keeper need not advance so far and could afford to be 10.5 yards (9.6 metres) from the attacker. For the narrowest angles the keeper can stand right off, confident, in theory at least, that he has everything covered.

All of this requires very fine judgement, especially the timing of the keeper's initial run. For central attacks there is really no choice. If the defence is beaten 30 yards (27 metres) out and the goalkeeper moves straight away he can smother the shot just past the penalty spot. If the defence is beaten further out, at 40 yards (37 metres), say, and the goalkeeper reacts immediately the critical position is reached just inside the penalty area. It could be argued that for these greater distances the goalkeeper should wait. To take the example just quoted, he could delay until the striker had closed the 30-yard point. Then the outcome would be exactly as before with a meeting just past the penalty spot. What is different? For a striker, crossing the edge of the penalty area with no threatening movement on the goalkeeper's part is psychologically very important. The shot is likely to come early, with the goalkeeper not yet in the prime position, and will be very confidently hit.

Things do not move much in the keeper's favour until the angle of attack has swung round to about 30 degrees to the goal line. The pitch markings then provide a rough guide: inside the lines joining the goalposts and the corners of the goal and penalty areas (Fig. 7.4) the keeper must run when the defence is beaten;

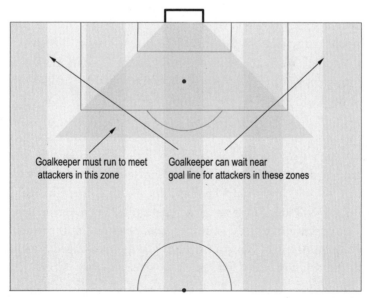

Fig. 7.4: Zones within which goalkeeper can run or wait in a one-on-one attack

for more acute angles he can afford to wait and need not advance so far to block the shot.

Good goalkeepers will always be thinking of the narrowed-angle position, moving almost intuitively to face the line of impending attack with a balanced position between the near and far posts. Defenders too: any defender who can get back into contention with the attacker should attempt to steer him away from the dangerous central positions and do as much as possible to delay a shot until the striker has run into the very acute-angle, less dangerous shooting positions.

A goal from the fourth set piece, the direct free kick, is of even higher probability. It is not possible to score from a single touch in an indirect free kick but the position is so easily transformed by a simple pass that in threatening positions both types of kick, direct and indirect, must be defended with a wall. Determining numbers for the wall at various distances and angles is not difficult; but first, a cautionary tale.

When a free kick is awarded, defenders invariably crowd the position to prevent its being taken quickly. The referee usually asks the striker, 'Do you want a wall?', which seems curious. Why should the striker opt for something that will lessen his chances of scoring? What the referee is really doing is using his discretionary powers in offering an advantage to the striker, who perhaps sees a gap he can exploit despite the positions of the attendant defenders. If the striker refuses a wall, then the referee indicates that the kick can be taken; he does not need to confirm this with a shattering blast of his whistle. This is exactly what happened when Arsenal's Thierry Henry scored his cheeky free kick in the important Premiership match with Chelsea in December 2004. At that stage Arsenal and Chelsea were in genuine contention for the number one position in the league, although Arsenal ultimately wilted. The most outraged member of the Chelsea team was their goalkeeper, Petr Cech, later admonished by the FA for his comments about the match referee, Graham Poll. Cech was at his far post, going through the complicated geometry of aligning the wall, thus leaving an enormous gap that Henry was able to exploit by taking the kick quickly. This underlines one of the most important principles of good defending: the goalkeeper should leave the far-post setting up to an outfield player, although he should call out how many defenders he wants in the wall. And he should watch the free kick position at all times.

If the striker accepts a wall, the referee will not give permission for the shot until it is in place and we then have the familiar spectacle of the referee pushing back four or more defenders whose ability to make a simple assessment of the required wall distance has mysteriously deserted them. Attackers cannot now work the advantage rule and conjure a scoring shot during this temporary mayhem. Many 'goals' have rightly been disallowed and free kicks ordered to be retaken under these circumstances. But let us assume that the wall will feature and defenders set it up properly. How many defenders are needed in each position?

In our study of the swerving free kick (Bray and Kerwin, 2003) we gave a formula for calculating this which produces the number of wall defenders for free kicks from various angles and distances. The predicted numbers correspond well with walls set up in actual matches. Most keepers position the wall with one side covering the far post and the other coming across just far enough to leave a clear sight of the shot (cf. Fig. 3.1). In practice about 75 per cent of the goal line is covered by the wall. The position is in many respects like that of the goalkeeper/attacker one-on-one, with a barrier apparently blocking the route for a straight shot. But a straight shot is seldom what elite kickers have in mind, and to someone who can strike the ball well with swerve there is a very inviting target to aim at, especially for free kicks in the central zones around the edge of the penalty area.

It is interesting to see how the wall shrinks as the point of the attack moves away from the central areas. In Fig. 7.5, the outer circle shows the position of a 30-yard (27-metre) free kick. The

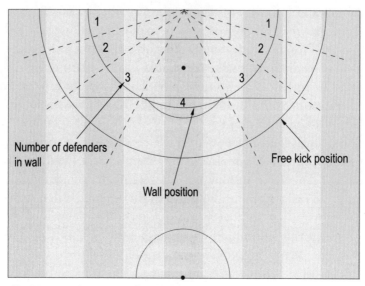

Fig. 7.5: 30-yard (27-metre) free kick showing number of defenders in wall for various angles of the kick

inner circle represents the positions at which the wall must form at the legal free kick distance of 10 yards (9.1 metres). For central free kicks it can be seen that 4 defenders are needed in the wall, but that the numbers drop as the angle of the kick becomes more acute. Closer to goal the numbers increase. Fig. 7.6 shows the requirements for a 20-yard (18.3-metre) kick with wall numbers rising to 5 for the dangerous central positions. Apart from the locations just inside the 'D', most of the free kick positions from 20 yards would be inside the penalty area. This case is included in Fig. 7.6 for completeness, the assumption being that these kicks inside the penalty area are indirect. This is unlikely in practice as most infringements in these positions would result in penalty kicks.

A central free kick from 20–30 yards (18–27 metres) may be very inviting but there is still a lot of work to be done. Let us assume that the striker can hit the ball with perfect sidespin, swerving it from right to left, and aims at the undefended half of

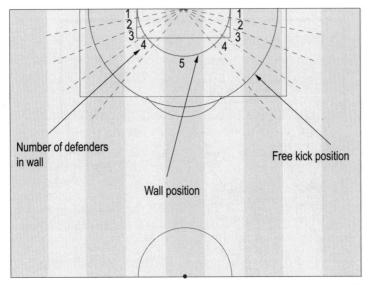

Fig. 7.6: 20-yard (18.3-metre) free kick showing number of defenders in wall for various angles of the kick

the goal shown in Fig. 3.1. If he starts the ball too far right, the keeper makes an easy save. He can start the ball a little to the left, and swerve it so that it crosses the goal line dead centre. Or at the other extreme, he can start it even further left, so that it finishes tucked just inside the far post. The undefended half of the goal line may seem very inviting, but to hit this target, relatively large at the goal line, the striker must keep the ball between narrow limits as it crosses the wall. This is because the swerve becomes greater and greater as the distance increases so a small error in position at the wall is magnified by the time the ball reaches the goal line.

It is no easier when the vertical dimension is considered: to get the ball down in time it must not cross the wall too high, which means tight control of the speed and elevation of the shot. In fact, the striker is attempting to slot the ball through a 'letter box' of extraordinarily small dimensions just above the wall. Fig. 7.7 shows the limits for a central free kick from 25 yards (23 metres).

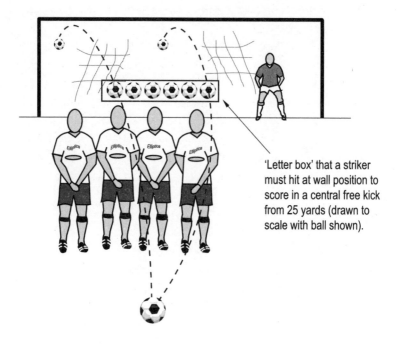

'Letter box' that a striker
must hit at wall position to
score in a central free kick
from 25 yards (drawn to
scale with ball shown).

Fig. 7.7: Central free kick from 25 yards (23 metres)

This target is just greater than 6 ball-widths. At 20 yards from
goal the striker's task is easier as the 'letter box' expands to just over
eight ball-widths. The shot becomes progressively more demanding,
though, as the kick swings round to more acute angles, since the
width of the 'letter box' rapidly reduces. Less than about 25
degrees to the goal line it is really not worth a direct shot and
playing the free kick to team mates in the form of a conventional
centre would be tactically more astute. If the striker can work a
bit of topspin magic into the delivery, prospects improve, at least
as far as keeping the ball down is concerned. Even better is the
Carr–Hunt special discussed in Chapter 3. The illegality of their
original free kick – when the ball had not travelled far enough
before it was hit again – is easily overcome by passing the ball a
short distance before it is flicked into the air so that the striker

can make contact, but this possibly demands too much precocity in today's game.

There are perhaps only two other significant issues related to direct free kicks. The first concerns extra protection for the goalie. Why not station defenders on the goal line, at each post, as for corner kicks? There are signs that some teams are prepared to experiment with this tactic. From the striker's point of view there are now many more bodies in the way of the shot so that the kick resembles its historical predecessor, a blast at goal, albeit with swerve, relying on a gap in the crowd of players or a chance deflection. For the defenders the obvious implication is that anyone stationed on the goal line simply plays all of the opposition onside. In many respects it is like a corner kick although the threat is now central, rather than from the side. Either way it is a risk and it will be interesting to see which tactic prevails in practice.

The second issue concerns attackers who join the defensive wall. Their intention is to unsight the goalkeeper, expanding the coverage beyond his intended limit, so shutting down his view of the kick completely and reducing his chances of making a save. There is nothing wrong with this as no rule states that the goalkeeper should have an unimpeded view of the ball in a free kick. Another intention of this practice is more sinister though. Watch any free kick and you will see how many times defenders are barged out of position, leaving a convenient gap in the wall for the striker to exploit. Referees might find it difficult to give a ruling in this case. Pushing normally relates to a player in possession of the ball and in a defensive wall no one is actually playing the ball. Perhaps it is a case of impeding the defender, but again, a defender in a wall is not really trying to reach the ball in a free kick. It is certainly unsporting behaviour, a punishable offence, but lots of pushing and shoving goes on in set pieces by both teams, usually on the referee's blind side.

The question was posed earlier in Chapter 3 but it is worth restating in the light of the above: is there such a thing as an unstoppable free kick? With suitable caveats about the skill of the striker, the answer is affirmative. We can see from the results of Fig. 7.7 just how demanding the challenge is in practice and even if the shot comes off only 15 per cent of the time, it is still a very remarkable achievement.

If set pieces are increasingly the mechanism for breaking dead-locked matches then penalty kicks are the absolute gold-standard way of achieving this. The shoot-out, too, however much it is deprecated by purists who would prefer drawn matches to be replayed, gives a fresh opportunity to resolve two hours of inconclusive play. Systems such as the 'golden goal' have been introduced in major competitions with the same purpose: a tie is effectively resolved immediately one side manages to score a goal in extra time. But such systems generally produce a kind of para-lysis, with neither team wishing to commit to all-out attack, so the issue often comes down to penalties once more. There is also the commercial imperative. Fixture congestion caused by unre-solved matches crowding into the scheduled run of games is simply not welcome in modern football because of the strain it places on team resources and the potential for injuries. Sponsors, from soft-drink vendors through to equipment manufacturers to television companies, also tend to like decisive outcomes.

I discussed the psychology of the shoot-out between Liverpool and AC Milan in Chapter 5. Milan was the better side in the first half, Liverpool in the second, then decisively Liverpool in the shoot-out. Justice is not always done in such an evident way, however. Most impartial observers who watched the 2005 FA Cup Final between Arsenal and Manchester United would agree that United were the better side throughout normal and extra time. The game ground on with Arsenal absolutely on the rack. But that team, no matter how poor their performance had been, knew then that they were just five kicks away from victory and approached the shoot-out in a better psychological frame of mind than United. Just one goal, Paul Scholes having missed a penalty for United, decided the tie and left United absolutely nothing to show for their season. Some may complain at the word 'missed' and argue that Arsenal's goalkeeper, Jens Lehmann, made a fabulous save. In truth no goalkeeper playing to the rules should get anywhere near the ball in a penalty, as we shall see. But first, let us be clear on the rules that govern this simplest free kick of all.

For many years the goalkeeper was obliged to stand on the goal line and was not allowed to move his feet until the instant of the kick. In football's earliest era some goalkeepers, imbued with the finest principles of sporting play, actually refused to make any attempt at a save, so shocking were deliberate offences in the penalty area. Times have changed. Nowadays, goalkeepers can move before the kick, but only if they remain on the goal line. A further curious feature of the rule states that keepers must face the kicker before the ball is played. There may be some deep-rooted historical explanation for this but it is hard to see how any advantage could be gained by using any other stance.

Shoot-outs differ from penalty kicks awarded in the normal course of a game in the sense that following up on a shot to score from a rebound from the goalkeeper is not permitted in a shoot-out. Even in a 'normal' penalty the striker is not allowed to play the ball a second time unless it has been touched by another player. Very often in conventional penalties, rebounds, whether from the goalkeeper, the goalposts or the crossbar, are converted by team mates who follow the kick into the penalty area, but even this course of action is excluded in the shoot-out. All designated penalty-takers must sweat it out in the centre circle until their turn arrives.

The antics of Bruce Grobbelaar and most recently Jerzy Dudek in influencing the outcome of the shoot-outs in Rome and Istanbul were described earlier, but these were not the first occasions when such tactics were applied. For many years goalkeepers have tried to destabilise penalty takers by attempting some verbal exchanges before the kick, and stories abound of the tactics used by players taking penalty kicks in the old days, when the ball sported a lace to close the casing after the rubber bladder had been inserted. It was *de rigueur* for the kicker to place this facing the goalkeeper so that the boot's contact with the ball would be unimpeded by this ugly intrusion. Some goalkeepers would walk out and turn the lace to face the kicker. There was nothing in the rules about this and it would, of course, be turned round again, but the goalkeeper had exercised some authority and the kicker's nerves would jangle a little more.

The penalty kick is the easiest set piece to analyse in the bio-mechanics of football. To build a model of the goalkeeper's dive, David Kerwin and I analysed detailed video images of repeated attempts at a save under match conditions and supplemented these by parallel measurements of the complex ground reaction forces as the goalkeeper dived from an instrumented force plate. By ensuring that the digital cameras could record a stereoscopic view of the action it was possible to obtain 3-D coordinates of the goalkeeper's movements and record the exact instant at which the ball crossed the goal line. In this way we determined the goalie's limits of reach (Fig. 7.8), no matter what angle of dive was used. As can be seen, it is not possible to reach the posts in a horizontal dive starting from the centre of the goal line because the goalkeeper cannot bring the powerful thigh and calf muscles into concerted action when diving horizontally. This is fully real-isable only in a vertical jump in which both legs are equally extended. There is also the problem of achieving adequate trac-tion between boot and ground for very flat dives. Keepers sometimes *do* get right across the goal line, but only by preceding the dive with a lateral step. So greater coverage is achieved at the expense of extended reaction time, not a good trade-off for a penalty save, unless the keeper guesses exactly right and moves early.

There is no guarantee that the ball will be saved even within the diving envelope, of course. It takes a finite time to complete the full diving action and a well-placed ball will be nestling in the back of the net long before the dive is complete. This is because

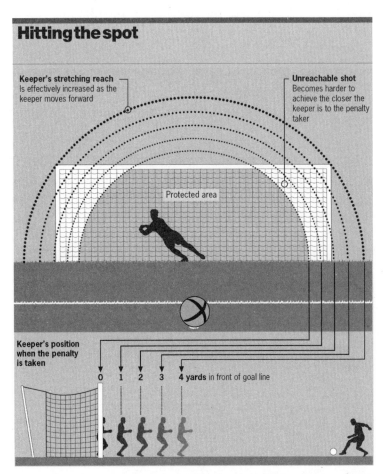

Hitting the spot

Keeper's stretching reach
Is effectively increased as the keeper moves forward

Unreachable shot
Becomes harder to achieve the closer the keeper is to the penalty taker

Protected area

Keeper's position when the penalty is taken

0 1 2 3 **4 yards** in front of goal line

Fig. 7.8: Goalie's diving envelope showing the unsavable zone (top graphic) and keeper's encroached positions (bottom graphic)

the flight time of a well-struck penalty is about half a second, and the goalkeeper's reaction time about half of this again. If the goalkeeper waits until the instant of the shot, his delayed reaction will mean that the ball will be half-way to goal. To have any chance of saving the shot the goalie must begin his dive before the ball is actually struck, perfectly legal provided he does not move off his line. There are many cues that professional goalkeepers use to predict the direction of the shot, one of the most reliable being the direction in which the penalty-taker's non-kicking foot is pointing at the instant of the kick. This was checked by Franks and Hanvey (1997) during Euro '96 and confirmed for more than 85 per cent of penalties. The same with the angle of the striker's hips (Williams and Burtwitz, 1993). If these are open, with the chest pointing towards the goalkeeper's left-hand post, this usually means that the striker will deliver the ball in this direction. If closed, the goalkeeper's right-hand post is the likely target. Acting on these cues by diving quickly in the direction of the shot maximises the chance of success, and as with a save in the goalkeeper/attacker one-on-one position, style is unimportant. A leg or arm extended in the last fraction of a second can result in a brilliant reaction save.

The kicker's aim should be to place the shot in the unprotected area of the goal, the 'unsavable zone' of Fig. 7.8 (top graphic), representing 28 per cent of the total goal area. Strikers can go close to the boundary, even a little inside it, confident that this is the absolute limit of the goalkeeper's reach. If this target seems too demanding, contrast the accuracy required with the precision placement needed in beating a defensive wall. Opinions also vary on the best type of kicking action, from a full-velocity instep kick to a more sedate but crisply struck side-foot placement. The former go wrong more often, usually resulting in shots that are blasted wide or over the bar.

Success in any kind of kicking depends on mastering the skill and being able to reproduce it. No player should arrive at the penalty spot with any doubt about the intended placement of the shot, so the exercise becomes one of repeating a familiar action rather than an untried, speculative effort. Practice is the key to success and penalties should be part of every serious training session, preferably at the end of a hard workout to replicate the physical and psychological demands of a two-hour match. The days are long gone when it could be admitted, as one England manager did after a spectacular failure in a shoot-out, that it was unnecessary to practise penalty taking.

Further tactics can be used to improve the overall success rate of the squad in a shoot-out. Research (McGarry and Franks, 2000) showed that if the weakest players take their penalties earliest in the sequence with the strongest last, there is a significant improvement in the overall chances of success. Inexperienced penalty takers are more likely to succumb to the performance-limiting effects of cognitive anxiety if their wait is unduly long. McGarry and Franks' report also drew attention to the strategic importance of key substitutes being used when matches remain deadlocked close to the end of extra time. There is no point in leaving experienced penalty-takers unused on the substitutes' bench when such individuals may be pivotal in deciding the outcome of the impending shoot-out.

Beyond achieving consistency of technique there is little more the kicker can do to improve the chances of success. Some of the more audacious players attempt to fool the goalkeeper by checking during the run-up, hoping that the goalie will commit to a dive, then sending the ball in the opposite direction. This requires nerve. But it is a different matter for the goalie. By moving forward (illegally) before the ball is struck, he can improve the chances of a save significantly. Fig. 7.8 (bottom graphic) shows how the goalie's effective coverage increases as he moves towards the kicker. This is simply analogous to 'narrowing the angle'. The undefended part of the goal is rapidly reduced and about 4 yards (3.7 metres) from the line his theoretical coverage blots out the whole area. Again there is no guarantee that a save will be made if the ball is played within the goalkeeper's theoretical reach, but an aggressive forward move before the ball is struck is very intimidating for the striker, who may just be unsettled enough to miss the target.

As already noted, this can be taken to extremes: in the 2003 European Cup final, Dida – AC Milan's goalie – took decisive if illegal action to break the deadlock in the shoot-out, advancing nearly to the edge of the goal area to save the penalty. Referees still seem to be very ambivalent about these tactics. This is curious since in senior competition the referee's assistant is tasked precisely with spotting encroachments. Perhaps it is time for a formal reminder of the rules. It is bad enough to lose a shoot-out after two hours' hard competition, infinitely worse if the deciding goal is a dubious penalty.

Analysing the placement of penalty kicks is a very effective way of improving overall tactics and technique. David Kerwin and I did this for England's last foray into the shoot-out, the quarter-final against Portugal at Euro 2004. The positions where the ball crossed the line (or missed the goal) are shown in Fig. 7.9 for the 14 penalties it took to resolve the encounter. Two, those of Rui Costa for Portugal and David Beckham for England, were wasted, full-velocity instep kicks that saw each shot sailing over the bar, at opposite sides of the goal. Of the remaining six, Portugal placed 5 of their penalties in the unsavable zone, and only one, an outrageous comedy kick by Helder Postiga, within the technically savable area. He nevertheless scored. The statistics show that England missed with only one of their remaining six, but a glance at Fig. 7.9 shows how technically naïve these penalties were. With the exception of Owen Hargreaves' well-taken kick, all were eminently savable. Three were hit straight down the middle and scored. The other two were not very far away, and it was inevitable, perhaps, that Darius Vassell's tentative shot would be the one that goalkeeper Ricardo gratefully scooped up.

Little is known about the intensity with which set pieces are rehearsed in the professional game. The greatest potential reward for even moderate skill – simply the ability to strike the ball with

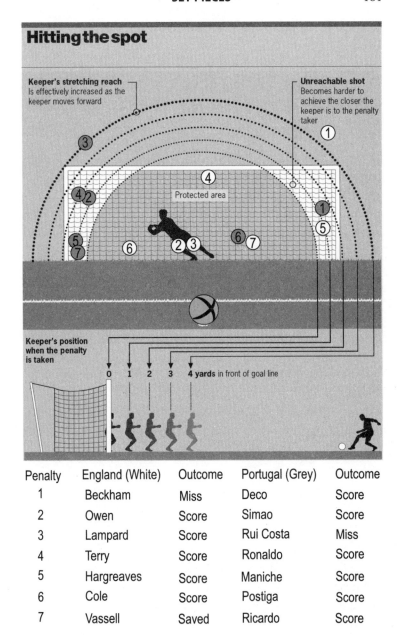

Fig. 7.9: England's performance in shoot-out against Portugal, Euro 2004 Championship

Penalty	England (White)	Outcome	Portugal (Grey)	Outcome
1	Beckham	Miss	Deco	Score
2	Owen	Score	Simao	Score
3	Lampard	Score	Rui Costa	Miss
4	Terry	Score	Ronaldo	Score
5	Hargreaves	Score	Maniche	Score
6	Cole	Score	Postiga	Score
7	Vassell	Saved	Ricardo	Score

reasonable speed into an undefended part of the goal – accrues from the penalty kick, and so it is surprising that teams often seem unprepared when this golden opportunity comes along. One of the simplest playing statistics to determine is individual players' conversion rates in penalty kicks, a figure that should be known from careful assessment in training. The ball should always go to the currently most successful player, injury not-withstanding, and not simply to the regular penalty-taker. Equally baffling is the fact that, with a shoot-out imminent, team coaches sometimes have to wander around cajoling players into taking penalties. What better indication of a player's mental state is there than reluctance to volunteer for a penalty? The remedy is practice under as realistic conditions as possible so that spot kicks become a repetition of a familiar skill and not an optimistic punt. The same goes for the other set pieces that have been discussed. Improvisation is a vital ingredient of football but not when careful practice and execution of a skill can offer better returns.

CHAPTER 8

UP IN THE AIR – READING FOOTBALL'S FUTURE

Forecasting the future can be misleading, and it is easily possible to be wrong 100 per cent of the time. This is especially true when the topic is football. Who could possibly have foreseen that a pastime for schoolboys would become the world's most popular game and that its exponents would rise from the level of hirelings, bought and sold like commodities in a demeaning transfer system as late as the 1960s, to become multi-millionaires today? Not much more than 50 years ago, the FA refused payment of top England internationals' expenses claims for taking taxis to match venues. They were admonished for not using public transport. Stanley Cullis, England international and later immensely successful as manager of Wolverhampton Wanderers, recalled, 'We were in a queue leading up to the underground railway (the Tube) at Wembley and I can recall standing in the queue, which was about a mile long from Wembley Stadium. The spectators who recognised us were nudging each other and informing their friends that so-and-so who'd been playing that day for England was having to take his turn in the queue . . . Oh, no, no, no, you certainly weren't allowed a taxi.' This is scarcely imaginable today, even as a fantasy; David Beckham, hanging off a strap in a crowded carriage, swapping stories with supporters en route to the new Wembley Stadium?

This look at the future then will be a cautious glimpse; not at what the game might be like in the next 150 years but at what is just around the corner in terms of scientific developments and what is likely to make an impression on today's generation of fans. Various themes emerge: ball and player tracking, and the technology to resolve disputed goals where the ball may or may not have crossed the line; the important topic of stress monitoring; an update on artificial pitches, now making a comeback in football; players' apparel, what they may soon be wearing in the form of playing strip, boots, shin guards and possibly head protection.

Goal-line technology is currently one of football's hottest topics. One of the best-known facts about football is that for a goal to be awarded the entire ball must cross the line. This can be difficult enough to judge when the ball is on the ground and can be clearly seen in relation to the goal line, but it becomes a near impossibility when the ball is in the air and there are no obvious reference points. There are many instances of legitimate goals being refused despite the ball having clearly entered the net. Three such incidents, one historic and two recent, will give a flavour of the problems that referees often face.

The first famously occurred during the 1966 World Cup final between England and West Germany, when England forward Geoff Hurst saw his shot cannon off the crossbar, strike the ground and rebound back into play. Swiss referee Gottfried Dienst seemed undecided but noticed that his linesman Tofik Bakhramov was flagging vigorously to attract his attention. A short conversation ensued; but in what language? Bakhramov was an Azerbaijani but was universally known afterwards in the media as 'the Russian Linesman', presumably because Azerbaijan was a satellite republic of the Soviet Union at the time. Perhaps football's universal language was sufficient. With much vigorous nodding of his head Bakhramov indicated a goal and that was Dienst's ruling, leaving the West German side feeling hard done by. Much reflection, research and debate over time has never satisfactorily resolved the issue of the validity of the goal and perhaps it never will be proven either way. England scored a fourth goal and effectively put the result of the match with West Germany beyond doubt. But in comparison, Liverpool's goal against Chelsea in an enormously important European Cup qualifier was the only one in the two-legged tie; not a comfortable way to decide such an important encounter.

Liverpool played that semi-final against Chelsea on 4 May 2005 for a place in the final later that month. Milan Baros was probably fouled by Chelsea's keeper Petr Cech, but Luis García for Liverpool picked up the rebound and shot at goal. Did Chelsea's defender William Gallas clear the ball before or after it crossed the line? As in the famous incident in the 1966 World Cup the referee appealed to his assistant, who confirmed the goal. Justice was probably done here as the alternative would almost certainly have been a red card for Cech, his sending-off and the award of a penalty.

Justice was not done, however, in a clear goal that was not awarded in the English Premiership match between Tottenham Hotspur and Manchester United on 4 January 2005. In the final minute the game was tied at nil–nil when Pedro Mendes of Spurs tried a 55-yard (50-metre) speculative shot. Roy Carroll, United's keeper, fumbled the ball, allowing it to bounce at least a yard over the line. He promptly scooped it back into play, while the crowd and millions watching on television howled their disapproval. Because on this occasion neither the referee nor his assistant had a clear view, the goal could not be awarded.

This incident was the final straw; it prompted Sepp Blatter, FIFA's president, to announce that technology to resolve such controversies would be speedily evaluated. When exploring each of these events a little more deeply it is possible to appreciate the challenges that such technology faces.

While no case can be made for Roy Carroll's 'save', in the sense that he would clearly have seen the ball bounce inside the net, defenders must sometimes be given the benefit of the

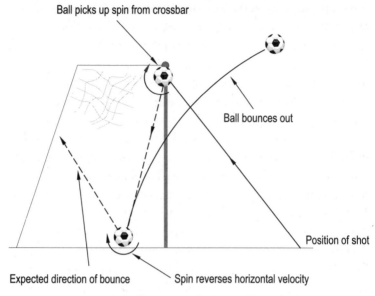

Ball picks up spin from crossbar

Ball bounces out

Position of shot

Expected direction of bounce

Spin reverses horizontal velocity

Fig. 8.1: Geoff Hurst's goal, 1966 World Cup final

doubt. It is not the defender's job to make a judgement of whether the ball is over the line or not in the split second it takes to head, kick or (in the goalkeeper's case) punch the ball clear. In Hurst's case however, without any defender's intervention at all, the ball entered the goal yet still bounced back into play. There have been numerous similar incidents over the years. Hurst's shot struck the bar off centre, with the ball's centre of mass below that of the crossbar (Fig. 8.1). We have already met this kind of impact in Chapter 6, where the dynamics of kicking were described. In these cases it is the ball that is moving and the crossbar (effectively the 'foot') that is at rest. Spin is the natural outcome, just as in kicking, but because of the rigidity of the crossbar and the enhanced frictional interface between the bar and the ball, the spin, as the ball is deflected downwards, is much greater. Downward impacts like these always produce backspin. As Fig. 8.1 shows, the angle of the second impact with the pitch would normally carry the ball further into the net, and there the matter would rest – an undisputed goal. But if the surface is dry, as it was during the 1966 final at Wembley that day, the frictional grip and the spin can be so great when the ball touches the surface that its horizontal velocity is reversed, and it bounces out. This is exactly what golfers achieve when they put so much backspin on a shot that the ball does not simply stop on landing on the green, but jumps backwards.

The problem with both kinds of incident in football – defender interceptions or spin-outs – is that they are over in the blink of an eye. For example, a ball moving at 25 metres per second could cross the line by the legal amount and be returned back into play within 18 milliseconds, so unless the officials are perfectly placed and actually looking at that instant, awarding a goal becomes a matter of guesswork. Video replays might seem at first glance to be the ultimate decider – after all, millions of television viewers gave their immediate verdict on the Carroll incident – but in practice the replay is not the perfect answer to the problem.

The first objection is that even the most carefully contrived camera locations rarely provide a continuously unimpeded view of the ball in relation to goal line, posts or crossbar. The image of the ball is frequently lost in the general mêlée when defenders and attackers naturally pack the goal area when the goal is under threat. The second point is that it takes a finite time for someone – the fourth official – to give a ruling. Such delays are tolerated in games such as American football or cricket where the play is frequently interrupted, but it would destroy Association football as a free-flowing spectacle. This is not to reject video replay in all its contexts. It is increasingly used, for example, to study violent incidents that occur on and off the pitch and can be vital in ensuring that transgressors do not go unpunished. What is needed in resolving goal-line disputes is something that can determine the ball's position continuously and accurately and is not affected by such inconvenient things as arms, legs or even goal posts that get in the way of conventional images. Enter position location, using high-frequency radio transmission.

For several years, three German organisations – the Fraunhofer Institute, Cairos Technologies and ball-maker Adidas – have been experimenting with a ball containing a microchip. This object is very light, measuring roughly 12 × 16 mm, and carries its own power supply. It works by sending out high-frequency radio bursts, 2,000 every second, which are used to fix its position very accurately in 3-D. The system also caters for the measurement of player positions using similar chips carried in the shin guards, but transmitting only 200 times per second.

The signals are picked up by fixed antennae, usually mounted on the floodlight assemblies around the stadium. High-frequency radio waves are not impeded by intervening objects such as human limbs or goal-posts so the problem of the ball being obscured as in conventional video imaging does not arise. And anyone concerned about the hazards of high-frequency radiation on players or spectators can be reassured. The signal power is only about 1/400 that of a mobile phone.

The ball's or player's exact position is automatically calculated by measuring the time it takes each signal from the embedded chip to arrive at the receiving antenna positions. If the signal speed is known (it is actually the speed of light) and also the time taken, working out the distance is very simple using the equation *distance* = *speed* × *time*. Since the speed of light is so great and the time intervals are extremely short, the signal processing needs to be very sophisticated. It is carried out on a small cluster of computers and continuously calibrated by using signals sent from reference transmitters at known positions. Because the ball is frequently substituted when it goes out of play, all those that feature in a match will need to be similarly equipped, and the measurement system automatically alerted whenever the ball is changed.

Having pinpointed the ball it is then only a matter of comparing its coordinates at each instant with those of the goal line, goal-posts and crossbar and arranging for some sort of signal to be triggered when the ball is over the line. Implicitly, the embed-ded microchip will need to reference the exact centre of the ball to facilitate this calculation. Just how this will be achieved is not known at the time of writing. It seems unlikely, for example, that the chip will bounce about freely inside the bladder. The system will also need to be robust to continue working reliably under the battering the ball receives in the course of an average game.

Assuming all this can be realised in a working system, how accurately can the ball be tracked? Since it transmits 2,000 times per second, a position is fixed every half-millisecond, and in this interval a ball kicked very fast, at 30 metres per second, will have moved just one and a half centimetres between readings. This accuracy is good enough to resolve goal-line incidents. For the kind of ball speeds encountered in football you might be out by a centimetre or so in arguing that the ball had completely crossed the line, but it is an enormous improvement on today's hit-and-miss methods. The other important benefit of the system is that it works in real time: there is no delay between the incident occurring and notification of the fact, so the game need not be interrupted while the officials go into a huddle. Exactly how the information will be relayed to the referee is not known at present. It could be declared publicly at a match by flashing a signal on the scoreboard so that players and spectators are aware of a goal having been scored. This raises the question of whether referees will be able to overrule the system. If some sort of infringement preceded the 'goal' this should clearly be the case, but, if not, on what grounds could a goal be refused? Referees may not feel com-fortable at having to surrender key decision-making to technology, but perhaps the positive message for the officials is that the mundane decisions – did the ball cross the line? did it go out of play? – will be handled automatically, leaving them free to give more important rulings.

The technology for goal-line incidents could be pushed fur-ther. Throw-ins or corner kicks are no more difficult to measure than disputed goals. It is just a question of comparing the ball's coordinates with those of the touchline or the dead-ball line. The thorny issue of offside might also be resolved once and for all. Many goals are allowed or refused in ambiguous circumstances because of the difficulty officials sometimes face in determining ball and player positions at the crucial moment.

Offside is easily tracked by microchip in principle, and determined on a very small amount of information: whether the attacker is closer to the opponents' goal line than the second-last defender and the ball. The problem is that over the years, accretions of meaning and qualifications have been piled on this deceptively simple rule so that it is sometimes difficult to see how offside decisions are made in practice. For example, the very latest interpretation of 'closer to' means 'any part of the head, body or feet, but excluding the arms'. The rationale is that because the ball cannot legally be played with the hands or the arms, these appendages cannot be offside. Then there are the issues related to 'active play', when someone technically in an offside position is interfering with play or an opponent, or is in some way gaining an advantage in being there.

Tracking any number of offside players using microchip technology is not a problem but, unlike the ball crossing the line for a goal, which is practically instantaneous, players tend to drift in and out of offside positions, perhaps interfering with play, perhaps not. If the tracking system continuously reported all such occurrences the referee would be very quickly swamped by information overload. Warning systems that give repeated false alarms tend to get switched off, so there may be some work to do before ball and player tracking improve offside decision-making.

Penalty kicks may offer more scope, but not in terms of whether penalties should be awarded in the first place. It would be easy to determine ball and player positions in relation to the penalty area using the new technology, but not to say with certainty where the actual offence occurred. Detecting illegal movement (encroachments) during the actual kick is feasible, though. The tracking system could determine whether the goalkeeper moved forward before the ball was kicked, which is all that the present version of the law requires. Penalty kicks could come to resemble the multiple restarts often seen in athletics when athletes jump the starter's gun, but, fortunately, football does have an escape clause. If any infringement occurs during or before a kick, but a goal nevertheless results, the rules say it must stand. Presumably we would only see repeat penalty kicks where the striker missed or the shot was saved following an illegal move.

FIFA chose a familiar way to test the microchip. A demanding trial of the technology took place in the same way that artificial playing surfaces were tested before they were given the green light. The system was evaluated at the World Under-17 football championship in Peru in September and October 2005, but the outcome was inconclusive and at the time of writing more technical evaluations were underway. A possible point of contention concerning eventual use of the microchip concerns the type of matches that will ultimately be approved. It is easy to see World Cup games, European Cup matches and those in the various national super leagues – English Premiership, Serie A in Italy and the German Bundesliga – going this way. But who will finance the installation costs for the minnows of world football? Perhaps we shall see dual standards in operation, with goal-line incidents being easily resolved at the grounds of the wealthy clubs but remaining a subject of human judgement and continuing controversy elsewhere.

For the players, there is both good and bad news. On the positive side the tracking system could very easily be adapted to provide a continuous read-out of heart rate in addition to positional information. Heart rate, as we have seen, is a good indicator of physiological stress, and a valuable means of determining when strain on the heart has risen to life-threatening levels. Players exhibiting distress symptoms would naturally be substituted before their condition became acute. There have been several tragedies that might have been averted with this kind of intervention. In 2005, Nedzad Botonjic, NK Ljubljana's goalkeeper, died in training, as did Hungarian Miklos Feher while playing for

Benfica in 2004. An equally tragic case occurred during the Confederations Cup held in France in 2003 when Marc-Vivien Foe, Cameroon's talented midfielder, collapsed during one of the tournament qualifiers and could not be revived. These were high-profile incidents. There may be more in the game's lower echelons and many potential tragedies may have been averted by fortuitous substitutions. FIFA's response has been to set up a medical research centre in Zurich to look into the causes of sudden heart failure among footballers. More effective medical screening will result and continuous monitoring of players' heart rate during competition is likely to gain widespread approval.

The players may not be so keen on the system's other more routine capabilities. By using tell-tale microchips in players' shin guards it would be very easy to assess the relative work-rates and quickly identify those individuals not pulling their weight. Metabolic distress would be a legitimate reason and lead to quick action, but for players simply avoiding their responsibilities there would be no hiding place. This leads to fascinating possibilities. We have already seen that defender, midfielder and attacker work-rates are different, but using this technology it should be possible to build up more detailed profiles; the holding midfielder, for example, working defensively just in front of the back 4, does not cover as much ground as his attacking partner. By comparing the observed and expected performances it will be possible to substitute players more strategically depending on the state of play at any particular stage of the game.

If players are to be substituted, either because of legitimate concern for their safety or to improve a team's playing performance, then, in addition to the match officials, coaches and medical staff would need access to the information. Some form of partitioning of the data would obviously be necessary. While it is quite proper for clubs to oversee the well-being of their own players, it is not ethical for them to have access to the opposition's performance data, or even, in the case of ball or player position monitoring, for them to be able to second-guess the referee's decisions.

For the sports scientists, detailed information on player and ball positions would provide a very rich database for post-match analysis, everything from assessment of the efficiency of playing formations right down to the level of detail that would make it possible to study the minutiae of free kicks: wall positions, ball speeds and aerodynamic forces. Such information would take match analysis to another level and would greatly improve scientific understanding of the game.

Goal-line monitoring may be awaiting final approval but artificial pitches were given the go ahead by FIFA in November 2004. Their origin in sport can be traced to a chance remark in an obscure report prepared for the Ford Foundation in the United States in 1961. This addressed the quality of educational facilities, including play areas. It concluded that these were so over-used in inner-city environments that surfaces were frequently reduced to bare earth, and children were unaware that traditional ball games were originally intended to be played on grass. The report presciently concluded that artificial surfaces were the solution and closed with a 'note to inventors: the non-educational market should be substantial'.

There was not exactly a rush to implement the findings, since no one knew how to manufacture artificial grass in the early 1960s. But the report came to the attention of the chemical group Monsanto, who saw the potential. They made a grass substitute by weaving extruded nylon fibres into a carpet and installed the first artificial pitch in 1964 in a school in Providence, Rhode Island. That might have remained just an experimental curiosity had it not been for a monumental show-stopper which occurred in Houston the following year.

In 1965 the Astrodome opened in the city to massive public acclaim. It was initially planted with a very hardy form of natural grass and Houstonians could watch football and baseball in air-conditioned comfort inside the 9-acre arena. This was not simply a concession to creature comforts: baseball had formerly been possible only as an evening spectacle, to avoid the 100 degrees Fahrenheit (38 degrees Celcius) daily temperatures in summer. So bad were the mosquitoes at the outdoor games that insect repellent was sold as freely as beer and hot dogs. There was just one snag with the new stadium, however. It was impossible to see the ball against the glare from the roof panels so these were lightly painted over. The grass, starved of natural light, promptly died. The venue might have been derided as simply a climate-controlled dustbowl, but rescue came when Providence's artificial pitch was described to the Astrodome's owner. Monsanto were contracted to turf the area with their product; originally called ChemGrass, it became universally known as Astro Turf after the job was finished. The original surface was not ideal, largely because the ball's bounce, influenced by the direction of the grain bristles in the nylon surface, was fast and unpredictable. This conferred a big home advantage to teams playing on plastic. There were also problems with injuries: the infamous 'carpet burn' associated with skin abrasions, as well as unpredictable traction leading to muscle and ligament damage. Nevertheless the technology seemed to offer advantages to Association football. Better understanding of the science of cultivation and treatment of grass, in addition to under-pitch heating, had made truly unplayable pitches a thing of the past – who nowadays would pay to watch world-class players struggling on the grassless, heavily sanded monsters of just a few decades ago? Artificial surfaces might take the game a step further, however, especially for those clubs finding it hard to keep playing surfaces in first-class condition throughout northern European winters.

The first artificial pitch in England was laid in 1971, and Queens Park Rangers began playing League games on an artificial surface in 1980, quickly followed by Luton Town, Preston North End and Oldham Athletic. There were immediate and obvious differences compared with grass. The ball zipped about and although players adapted by using different boots to help with balance in running and turning, there were still injury concerns. Skin abrasions and ligament and muscle damage aside, there was the issue of surface impacts. It was felt that the substrate of the pitch provided less 'give' than grass and soil, potentially dangerous in the case of head and limb impacts with the ground. That great British standby, a committee of investigation, was pressed into service in 1985, to consider the merits and disadvantages of artificial surfaces.

Headed by Sir Walter Winterbottom, the former England manager, the committee worked with commendable thoroughness and looked at three key aspects: ball/surface interaction, player movement and player/surface interaction, all assessed for natural as well as artificial surfaces, so that valid comparisons could be made. Meanwhile, as a precaution, a three-year moratorium was placed on further installations in England until the committee reported.

The ball's interaction with the surface was investigated using rebound and rolling resistance tests. The ball's rebound was higher on the artificial surface by between 3 and 6 per cent. But almost the same variation in bounce could be observed when ball pressure was varied by the amounts allowed in the regulations, or by using different balls of the same make, inflated to the same pressure. Rolling resistance, the frictional drag that causes the ball to lose speed as it moves across the surface, was significantly different, however, about 20 per cent less compared with grass.

Player movement was simulated by using a plate in which studs were inserted. This artificial 'boot' could be pressed into the surface, then gradually rotated to the point where it would slip. This simulated twisting in running. Sliding friction, typical of starting or stopping, was investigated by applying increasing horizontal force to the studded plate, noting the point at which it first moved. These tests were inconclusive in the sense that the particular type of stud patterns used affected the outcome more than the surface nature itself.

Finally player/surface interaction was examined by using a magnificent object called the 'Stuttgart Artificial Athlete', a mechanical device that simulates impact forces when running.

This is an important property; a surface with a good 'feel' will absorb upwards of 70 per cent of the energy involved in the impact. If it absorbs much less, as it will when the surface is hard and unyielding, injuries are likely. Conversely, a softer pitch absorbing more energy than the 70 per cent figure leads quickly to fatigue. Not much difference was observed between plastic and grass for simulated running in Winterbottom's assessments, but impact tests modelling collisions between an experimental head and the ground were of more concern. Impact force was demonstrably greater on artificial turf, essentially because the substrate, being less compressible, had poorer shock-absorbing properties than a grass and soil combination.

Publication of the report in 1989 ended the flirtation with artificial surfaces in the English game, the material being banned for 'high-level' League football, but allowed for lower-level competition where economics were important. Prior to Winterbottom's findings it had been said that the surface did not suit the English game, although what characteristic critics had then in mind was not revealed. Perhaps it was the pitch's greater liveliness both in terms of bounce and roll, properties which would have threatened that most English of tactical weapons, the long ball. In fact there was little in Winterbottom's report that really supported this disquiet; a lively pitch, natural or artificial, is easily subdued by selective watering. More pertinent might have been the fact that the surface could not at that time match the qualities of the best natural turf. Whatever the real issues, FIFA endorsed Winterbottom's findings and decreed that all international games would be played on grass. So that was that.

But elsewhere there were powerful reasons why artificial pitches had to be introduced if football was to be played as a winter game. One of the trail-blazers was Norway, whose first artificial pitch was laid in 1977. In the far north of that country the growing season for grass is limited to just a month, and few locations in Norway and countries at that latitude have a growing cycle as long as the football season. In 1984, before

Winterbottom's study, the Norwegians carried out their own research and came up with an acceptable product, the performance of which was much closer to that of a natural surface. There are now more than 150 artificial pitches in Norway and top players train exclusively on this material in autumn, winter and spring.

Probably the single most important factor in rehabilitating artificial turf has been the change in the material used to make the artificial grass fibres. The new material, polyethylene, is softer than nylon, yet still strong and elastic. Moreover, by in-filling the 'grass' filaments with a mixture of sand and granulated rubber, the impact properties can be improved and the surface made more akin to its natural counterpart. All of these developments prompted another look in 2001 by FIFA, who issued a 'Quality Concept' for artificial turf that year. Artificial pitches have now been sanctioned for international matches although major tournaments will still be played on grass. FIFA has also published a very comprehensive set of standards to which such artificial surfaces must conform. These address all of the Winterbottom issues, and more. For example, recoil is specified for both vertical and oblique impacts, the latter ensuring that the ball rebounds as predictably for angled impacts as it would from natural turf. In FIFA's accreditation system, approval follows not just acceptable performance of the surface material in a battery of tests but also measurements on pitches themselves, in various locations over the surface, to ensure that it has been correctly laid.

FIFA's scheme has been in operation for several years and over 80 artificial pitches have been installed worldwide, many by clubs who use artificial surfaces for their training grounds. Some were installed as pilot projects with substantial UEFA subsidies (nearly €200,000), including those of Dunfermline Athletic, FC Torpedo Moskva, SV Austria Salzburg and Orebro SK in Sweden. If there seems to be a northern bias, that is intentional: clubs in northern Europe find it especially difficult to fulfil European senior competitions during winter. This leaves their competitors, playing under more benign conditions, with an interesting dilemma: whether playing a key game on an unfamiliar artificial surface is preferable to the fixture congestion that occurs when matches are postponed because the opposition cannot deliver a playable pitch.

Artificial surfaces are likely to become more widespread. European clubs in the top flight will need to ensure their game does not suffer on plastic so we can expect many more to fall into line, perhaps by going for training grounds equipped with the new material. Most residual concern seems to be confined to the players, some of whom still distrust plastic and its apparently greater injury potential. They may or may not be reassured by UEFA's latest statistics: muscle and ligament injuries on the present generation of artificial pitches are 3.2 per 1,000 playing hours, compared with 7.6 per 1,000 playing hours for grass.

As usual the imperatives may all be economic. A modern artificial surface has an estimated life of 8 years, some sources claiming even 10–12. Operating costs are also impressive: it is cheaper by a factor of between 10 and 20 to maintain an artificial pitch compared with a grass one. It can also be played on continuously – very useful in an era where ground-sharing is becoming more common. Equally important, grounds can be hired out for community use with little fear that the surface will suffer. Contrast this with the Amsterdam Arena and similar stadiums where steep terracing or even partial enclosure means that the pitch has to be relaid in natural grass up to four times a year. In the end, money talks.

Playing apparel, money-spinning replica shirts apart, may appear to have little more to offer to improve the game. We tend to laugh at the strip worn by players of the Victorian era: baggy shorts drooping below the knee, heavy shirts and unwieldy boots. In doing so we forget that football was emphatically a winter sport, played much more often on heavy mud than grass. In the public school era of football in the early decades of the nineteenth century the players wore objects called 'navvies', boots fitted with iron tips to facilitate the brutal process of hacking. They mimicked the footwear worn by the hardy labourers, the 'navigators', who drove the railway and canal network throughout industrial Britain.

It will be recalled that when the England team of the 1950s met the Hungarians they scoffed at the apparently flimsy footwear the latter wore. The English boot that succeeded the brutal 'navvies' was unchanged for many years and had much more to do with the ability to heft a muddy lump of leather some distance than with aesthetics. The studs were nailed into a virtually rigid leather sole, and part of wearing-in a new pair involved hammering flat any nails that penetrated inside, enabling the boots to be worn in comfort. They covered the ankles and sported enormous toe caps. Generations of schoolboys were exhorted to kick the ball with the instep rather than the toe. But what was the point of a reinforced toe cap if not to facilitate that most basic of kicking actions, the toe-ender? It is doubtful whether much refined instep kicking could in any case occur, given the constraining effect of the high-sided boots and the lack of mobility of the ankle joint.

Actually, many innovations were under way even when England and Hungary were striding out at Wembley with their contrasting footwear. Adi Dassler, the German founder of the Adidas Company, was experimenting not just with lighter-weight boots but with detachable studs that were screwed, rather than hammered, into the soles. These proved their worth in the 1954 World Cup final between West Germany and Hungary. A downpour just before the game left the pitch in a treacherous condition, but Dassler was able to replace the Germans' studs with longer ones that ensured better traction. Following Germany's unexpected victory, few professionals wanted to play at succeeding tournaments in other than the Adidas model.

Dassler's boots offered not just improved mobility of the foot but also a very large weight reduction: his boots were nearly 50 per cent lighter than the earlier types. Since then there have been many innovations in boot design, but all have evolved in response to the demands the modern game places on players and the skills they are expected to display. The boot must absorb the shock of running but at the same time produce just the right amount of friction to prevent unintended slipping. The relevant forces can be measured using force plates with sufficient precision to reveal how the various forces change through the running cycle, from the boot's first contact with the ground to the point where it lifts off in completing the stride. The typical vertical force peaks at around two and a half times body weight, while the horizontal force is about a quarter of this. The horizontal frictional force changes direction, as it must in the cycle of running. Friction prevents the foot skidding when the boot is first planted, then assists it by acting in the opposite direction as the foot pushes the body forwards. A well-designed boot will accommodate vertical and horizontal forces by using insoles that distribute the load uniformly. Poor cushioning or badly configured stud patterns can act as stress concentrators, ultimately injuring the foot. In this regard the traditional six-stud pattern, which is not very effective in load distribution, is giving way to designs involving greater numbers distributed more scientifically around the sole. It is probably true that sponsorship deals mean that the game's stars seldom pay for the boots that they wear; just as well, as studies also show that boots undergo roughly three times as much punishment in training compared with match play, so regular replacement is an important consideration.

So much for the boot in relation to the player and the pitch; what about the equally important interaction with the ball? Fleeting as this contact is, everything that occurs in the resulting flight is determined by the interaction between a few square centimetres of the respective surfaces, compressed together then released in less than 10 milliseconds. One of the earliest innovations involved improvement of the frictional interface between boot and ball so that swerving the ball became a skill much more under the player's control. Little could be done regarding the ball itself; its inherent surface friction is determined to a large degree by the seams formed between the stitched panels, although rain and surface water from the pitch often act as unwanted lubricants.

The boot now became the focus of design improvements for frictional contact. The first design patents were taken out for a boot produced by the Englishman Jack Danks, who worked on his 'Eagle' design in 1983. He was said to have been led to the concept by studying the thin, synthetic rubber surfaces applied to table tennis bats for the same purpose. The principle was incorporated in his design in the form of 'rubber assistance pads' applied to the instep and outside of the boot. By increasing grip on the ball in this way it is not just spin control that is enhanced. The accuracy of straight deliveries such as long passes is also improved by ensuring that the ball is gripped more securely during the contact phase. Momentum is generated along the line of the intended kick with less likelihood of annoying deviations caused by the boot skidding on the ball's surface at the instant of impact. Danks' designs were later extended to apply to a detachable sleeve that would slip over the front of any boot, fulfilling the same function as the permanent friction layers.

Both concepts were independently evolved by former Liverpool player Craig Johnston. His design is embraced in the Adidas 'Predator' boot and since its emergence in 1993 many of the elite free kick artists in the game such as David Beckham and Zinedine Zidane have exploited its properties. In 2003 Johnston was narrowly beaten to the coveted 'Designer of the Year' award for his second innovation. His version of the detachable sleeve is registered as 'The Pig' and can be worn over a conventional boot. He apparently chose this name because when the surface of the sleeve impacted, then gripped the ball, the noise was reminiscent of a pig's squeal. What players feel about this animal accompaniment to their shots is not recorded, but defenders should take note. The frequency of the shriek should be roughly proportional to the spin applied, which is perhaps why really devastating free kicks are known as 'screamers' in the trade. Design trends for footwear will follow the changing nature of the game, but the overriding requirement will be for comfort and injury prevention. Not much protection can be offered for the ankle with the modern boot, but more scientific design of stud patterns will aid traction and help to prevent muscle and ligament damage caused by slips and skids on treacherous surfaces. Artificial pitches should in theory cause no problems concerning grip with conventional boots and studs, but there is a residue of disquiet among some players, who despite the contrary statistics are concerned about the risk of injury. These concerns may prompt another look at boots specially made for artificial surfaces, although designers are not likely to follow the pattern of the 1970s. Studs were dispensed with because of the unyielding nature of early plastic pitches and soles more often resembled the surfaces found on today's conventional trainers.

Compared with the research effort committed to footwear, the strip – the shirts and shorts – has received less scientific attention. It is ironic that most of the investment in the football strip is committed to visual design, later reproduced for replica shirts, a very big money-earner for the clubs. Many clubs have been criticised for the frequency with which the team strip is changed and not a few fans have wondered which team to cheer as the sides run out in unfamiliar strips at the start of the new season. Things are changing though in terms of the scientific research committed to the environmental and safety performance of the footballer's kit.

Football is played under widely varying climatic conditions. If the game is to continue expanding its international popularity then major tournaments must follow the new fan bases and markets. Little objection is nowadays raised to World Cup tournaments played in Mexico, the first of which in 1970 caused controversy because of the punishing effect of the combination of heat and altitude. Another difficult set of environmental conditions was found at the last World Cup, in 2002 in Japan and Korea, where it was not uncommon for temperatures to reach 77–86 degrees Fahrenheit (25–30 degrees Celsius) in combination with humidity levels as high as 79 per cent. Under these conditions, sweating – the body's temperature regulation mechanism – is greatly inhibited and fatigue sets in rapidly unless something is done.

The obvious solution in hot, humid conditions is to improve the skin's surface evaporation, something easily achieved by enhancing forced ventilation rates in the clothing worn. Cellular fabric is effective and also lighter than conventional material, but the required porosity means that skin shows through, spoiling the appearance of the strip. For this reason many players took to wearing a sweat-absorbing vest in the team's colours under a better-ventilated top. This principle has been incorporated in many commercial designs, based on multi-layered materials. The skin-adjacent layer is the same colour as the shirt but its main purpose is to be very effective in transporting sweat outward; this is achieved by using fibres of a precise size combined with fine powder coatings, the whole acting as a very efficient moisture conductor. The outer layer of the shirt can then incorporate large mesh panels front and back so that ventilation is enhanced.

The ideal would be for the complete ensemble of shirts, shorts and socks to be environmentally responsive, so that the fabric's intrinsic evaporation or insulation properties would change automatically in response to the external factors and the particular stresses of the game. The technology to achieve this is not very far away. It is also no exaggeration to say that prototypes – smart fabrics – have reached the stage where they can perform as wearable computers. In one case a lightweight material has been developed for medical purposes, which can accurately monitor respiration and heart rates, another approach to determining metabolic stress. Currently valued simply as a money-spinner, a replica shirt could also become a life-saver on the pitch.

Injuries are mostly related to the action of tackling, and while the humble shin guard will not prevent severe injury in the form of fractures it can protect players from damaging impacts in the form of kicks or the kind of raking injuries that result when studs are dragged painfully across the shin. FIFA have made the wearing of shin protection mandatory but generations of schoolboys were there first. They found that school exercise books doubled as shin guards as they were of just the right size and flexibility to wear inside the front of the socks.

Modern designs are more sophisticated and less of a threat to school homework. The best-performing types are made from a thermoplastic outer layer shaped to follow the shin's contours, cushioned by a second layer made of shock-absorbing material such as ethylene vinyl acetate (EVA). The function of the outer layer is to distribute the surface loading so that the inner layer may more effectively cushion it.

Research by Lees and Cooper in 1995 entailed dropping a known weight from a given height on to shin guards of various types attached to an experimental leg. Determining the deceleration of the weight after impact gave a measure of the shock absorbency of the material. Decelerations of between 28 and 56 per cent were found when the shin guard was used for protection compared with dropping the weight on to the unprotected leg. These tests confirmed the superiority of thermoplastic outer shells with EVA shock-absorbing layers. Work by Ankrah and Mills in 2003 entailed very detailed modelling of the impact between a simulated kick and the shin guard. These authors' results have suggested that the current European standard for shin guards is insufficiently stringent as it is based on too low an energy for the strength of a typical kick. This is an important finding, since impacts are frequently concentrated in a single stud of the boot. Such impacts intensify the instantaneous forces and under high point-loading, the outer layer of the shin guard may be completely ineffective in spreading the energy of the impulse. Any kind of protection is better than none at all, but there is scope for improvement in this basic object.

While no one would advocate playing without shin protection in today's game, it would be a brave person who tried to make a case for helmets. Heading may be judged safe but accidental clashes of heads, collisions with goal-posts or impacts with feet are not uncommon. Goalkeepers are most prone to injury caused by the latter and the case for head protection may be advanced first for the goalie. Or perhaps the innovation will emerge first in the junior game, where any action leading to potential injury to the head should be treated seriously. Heading in particular is a skill that needs to be carefully developed to ensure that the right techniques are ingrained before progression to the full-sized ball occurs. Lightweight helmets might have a lot to contribute here.

Despite the pitfalls of over-ambitious forecasting there are a couple of ways in which football is changing that are too tempting to overlook. The unexpected developments that make the greatest impression are not perhaps the game's affluence, the disparity between the richest clubs and players and the rest, its international popularity, nor even football's technical advances. These changes would not surprise any founding member of the Football Association if he were able to observe the game today, given Victorian enterprise and the love of technological innovation. The greatest shock to such a person might lie instead in two emerging factors that will move the game on in unexpected ways. These are the strength and popularity of women's football, unthought-of in 1863, and the mutation of the offside rule, now almost impenetrable in its complexity, with no discernible benefit to the game, the players or spectators.

As I write, women's football is reportedly the fastest-growing sport in the world, and its influence is now being felt at an international level. The FIFA Women's World Cup of 1999 was played in the United States before crowds of more than 90,000 spectators and in 2005 over 21,000 people watched the Euro 2005 Championship final in England. Large crowds for women's football are not unusual. In 1920, 53,000 spectators crammed into Everton's ground to see the elite women's team of the day, Dick-Kerr's Ladies, defeat their closest rivals, St Helen's Ladies. Dick-Kerr was a factory in Preston and the women formed up originally to play against the men's side. The FA's response to the women's game of the 1920s was characteristic. They banned women's teams from FA-affiliated grounds and the game was strangled.

Accounting for the success of women players is not difficult. At the elite level they can compete successfully in today's high-tempo conditions. They exercise at about 70 per cent of their maximal oxygen uptake, compared with 75 per cent for men, with total energy expenditures under match conditions around 80 per cent of their male counterparts. As we have seen, not all positional roles place the same energy demands on the players. Women may not yet contest possession with the same intensity as men in midfield but the best women could be very effective strikers for what are currently all-male teams. One Mexican woman player, Maribel Domínguez, very nearly achieved this. She was all set to join the Mexican second division club Atlético Celaya in 2004, having scored nine goals for the Mexican women's team at the Athens Olympics that year. Her hopes were dashed when FIFA quashed the move at its 2004 meeting in Zurich, ruling that '. . . there must be a clear separation between men's and women's football'. FIFA's intentions in maintaining segregated football are clear, but exactly what is meant by the word 'separation' if we interpret this in terms of ability and skill? In fact, FIFA's notions on what might assist the development of women's football have not been very enlightening. In 2004 Sepp Blatter, president of FIFA, suggested, 'Let the women play in more feminine clothes like they do in volleyball. They could, for example, have tighter shorts. Female players are pretty, if you excuse me for saying so, and they already have some different rules to men – such as playing with a lighter ball.' Blatter's counterpart Lennart Johansson, president of UEFA, voiced similar contentious opinions at the conclusion of a highly successful women's Euro 2005 Championship. 'Companies could make use of a sweaty, lovely looking girl playing on the ground, with the rainy weather. It would sell,' he told the BBC. The women wisely dismissed these remarks and corrected Blatter on his misconceptions about the ball they use. It is of regulation weight and size – in all respects the same as that used in the men's game.

Offside, now an obsolete concept, has no gender implications but its course has just as surely run as the old-fashioned views of FIFA and UEFA. The earliest definition meant anyone in front of the ball was offside. In today's version of the rule, arms and hands cannot be offside, because it is illegal to play the ball with these appendages, but everything else goes into the equation, from the decision of when the ball was last played to whether players technically offside are interfering with the game or not. Before the FA's earliest and highly restrictive definition was written into the famous 14 rules, the first Sheffield clubs, whose pedigree was as respectable as that of any of the FA's founding members, had no offside. The trend over the last 150 years has been to favour attackers, but at the expense of piling increasing complexity into the definition. Imagine the logical hurdles the officials must surmount in giving a split-second ruling. When was the ball last played? Where exactly is the suspect player (excluding hands and arms) in relation to the last two defenders? Are those other players active or passive, in other words interfering with play or not? It is a nightmare and it is quite legitimate to ask what it would cost to abandon offside – in fact, to give recognition to the position we have almost reached today. Put simply, defenders would have to do their jobs, to mark players and spend less time worrying about the intricacies of moving up at just the right instant to spring the offside trap. And attackers could concentrate on scoring goals, not manipulating the ambiguities of 'interfering with play', whatever this means. It would be a great relief for referees and their assistants, who could get on with controlling more meaningful aspects of the play.

It seems likely that within a decade mixed teams will be

playing football under the regulations and offside will have been scrapped. No doubt FIFA will restrict mixed football to minor competitions initially, and only a few women will break into the professional game; but in the end they will prevail. Similarly, the abandonment of offside will be subject to typically cautious evaluation, just as with goal-line technology and artificial pitches, but common sense will win through. We will witness a new era of tactical play, similar to that in the early twentieth century, as teams and coaches adjust formations to the new playing environment.

Football will be the better for both changes. In scrapping offside the game will regain its true attacking dimension and rediscover the single most important aspect of play: scoring goals. And with the growth of the women's game, football will recover a little of its soul, lost in the last two decades' rush for television revenues, club merchandising and the win-at-any-cost approach of some teams and players. With changes like these the beautiful game can only continue to prosper.

BIBLIOGRAPHY

Ankrah, S. and Mills, N. J. 'Performance of football shin guards for direct stud impacts', *Sports Engineering*, 6, 4, pp. 207–220, 2003.

Apter, J. H. 'The experience of being violent', paper presented at the Eighth International Conference on Reversal Theory, University of East London, 1997.

Bate, R. 'Football chance: tactics and strategy', in T. Reilly, A. Lees, K. Davids and W. Murphy (eds.), *Science and Football*. E. & F. N. Spon, pp. 293–301, London, 1988.

Bray, K. 'Simulation of goalkeeping strategies in Association football', in H. T. A. Whiting (ed.), *Readings in Sports Psychology*, pp. 258–267, Henry Kimpton Publishers, London, 1972.

Bray, K. and Kerwin, D. G. 'Modelling the flight of a soccer ball in a direct free kick', *Journal of Sports Sciences*, 21, 75–85, 2003.

Bray, K. and Kerwin, D. G. 'Modelling the long throw in soccer using aerodynamic drag and lift', in M. Hubbard, R. D. Mehta and J. M. Pallis (eds.), *The Engineering of Sport 5*, vol. 1. International Sports Engineering Association, pp. 56–62, Sheffield, 2004.

Brian Glanville. *The Story of the World Cup* (revised edition), Faber and Faber, London, 1997.

Cohen, J. and Dearnaley, E. J. 'Skill and judgement of footballers in attempting to score goals', *Brit. J. Psychol.* 53, 1, pp. 71–88, 1962.

Davey, C. P. 'Psychological assistance for footballers', in T. Reilly, A. Lees, K. Davids and W. Murphy (eds.) *Science and Football*, E & F. N. Spon, pp. 519–530, London, 1988.

Deloitte & Touche Sport: *Annual Review of Football Finance*, 2005.

Fazey, J. and Hardy, L. 'The inverted "U" hypothesis: a catastrophe for sports psychology?', *British Association of Sports Sciences Monograph 1*, National Coaching Foundation, Leeds, 1988.

Franks, A. I. and Hanvey, T. 'Cues for goalkeepers', *Soccer Journal*, pp. 30–38, 1997.

Gerisch, G. and Reichelt M. 'Computer and video-aided analysis of football games', in T. Reilly, J. Clarys and A. Stibbe (eds.), *Science and Football II*. E. & F. N. Spon, pp. 167–173, London, 1993.

Grant, A. G., Williams, A. M. and Reilly, T. 'Analysis of goals scored in the 1998 World Cup', *Journal of Sports Sciences*, 17, 826–827, 1999.

Hughes, M. D., Robertson, K. and Nicholson, A. in T. Reilly, A. Lees, K. Davids and W. Murphy (eds.), *Science and Football*, E. & F. N. Spon, 363–367, London, 1988.

Jan Ekstrand, Jon Karlsson and Alan Hodson. *Football Medicine* (revised edition), Martin Dunitz, London, 2003.

John H. Kerr. *Rethinking Aggression and Violence in Sport*, Routledge, Abingdon, 2005.

Lees, A. 'Biomechanics applied to soccer skills', in T. Reilly and A. Mark Williams (eds.), *Science and Soccer* (second edition), Routledge, pp. 109–119, London, 2003.

Lees, A. and Cooper, S. 'The shock attenuation characteristics of soccer shin guards', in G. Atkinson and T. Reilly (eds.), *Spree, Leisure and Ergonomics*, E. & F. N. Spon, pp. 130–135, London, 1995.

Luhtanen, P. H. 'A statistical evaluation of offensive actions in soccer at World Cup level in Italy 1990', in T. Reilly, J. Clarys and A. Stibbe (eds.), *Science and Football II*. E. & F. N. Spon, pp. 215–220, London, 1993.

Matt Jarvis. *Sport Psychology*, Routledge, London, 2002.

Mc Crudden, M. and Reilly, T. 'A comparison of the punt and drop-kick', in T. Reilly, J. Clarys and A. Stibbe (eds.), *Science and Football II*. E. & F. N. Spon, pp. 362–366, London, 1993.

McGarry, T. and Franks, I. M. 'On winning the penalty shoot-out in soccer', *Journal of Sports Sciences*, 18, 401–409, 2000.

Messier, S. P. and Brody, M. A. 'Mechanics of translation and rotation during conventional and handspring soccer throw-ins', *International Journal of Sports Biomechanics*, 2, 301–315, 1986.

Mike Hughes and Ian Franks. *Notational Analysis of Sport*, E. & F. N. Spon, London, 1997.

Morris Marples. *A History of Football*, Secker & Warburg, London, 1954.

Pain, M. A. and Harwood, C. G. 'Knowledge and perceptions of psychology within English soccer', *Journal of Sports Sciences,* 22, 813–826, 2004.

Partridge, D. and Franks, I. M. 'A detailed analysis of crossing opportunities from the 1986 World Cup', *Soccer Journal,* May / June 47–50; June/July 45–48, 1989 a, b.

Plagenhoef, S. *The Patterns of Human Motion*, Prentice-Hall, New Jersey, 1971.

Rahnama, N., Reilly, T. and Lees, A. 'Injury risk associated with playing actions during competitive soccer', *Br. J. Sports Med.,* 36, 354–359, 2002.

Reep, C. and Benjamin, B. 'Skill and chance in Association football', *Journal of the Royal Statistical Society, Series A,* 131, 581–585, 1968.

Reilly, T. and Ball, D. 'The net physiological cost of dribbling a soccer ball', *Res. Q. Exerc. Sport,* 55, 267–271, 1984.

Reilly, T. and Thomas, V. 'A motion analysis of work-rate in different positional roles in professional football match-play', *Journal of Human Movement Studies,* 2, 87–97, 1976.

Rogan Taylor and Andrew Ward. *Kicking and Screaming: An Oral History of Football in England*, Robson Books, London, 1995.

Tait, P. G. 'On the path of a rotating spherical projectile', *Transactions of the Royal Society of Edinburgh*, 16 (part 2), 491–506, 1896.

Thomas Reilly and A. Mark Williams (eds.). *Science and Soccer* (second edition), Routledge, London, 2003.

Van Gool, D., Van Gerven, D. and Boutmans, J. 'The physiological load imposed on soccer players during real match-play', in T. Reilly, A. Lees, K. Davids and W. Murphy (eds.), *Science and Football*, E. & F. N. Spon, pp. 51– 59, London, 1998.

Williams, A. M. and Burwitz, L. 'Advance cue utilisation in soccer', in T. Reilly, J. Clarys and A. Stibbe (eds.), *Science and Football II*. E. & F. N. Spon, pp. 239–244, London, 1993.

INDEX

Numbers in italics indicate Figures.